Dr. Allen's book is an insigh
music community. Dr. Allei

(aka "Classical" music) and relates the experiences of his young
developmental years with candor, eloquence and historical insight.
His sidebars add to the historical significance of his interviews.

Allen's book is a must read even if one is not a native of Philadelphia
but has a keen interest in American music from an Urban perspective.

Ellis L. Marsalis, Jr
Professor Emeritus
University of New Orleans

In George Allen's autobiography, *I Was Not Asked*, he reveals the
incredible journey of a black man who was determined not to
allow the ills of discrimination, racism, poverty, or disease to deter
him from reaching his goal of being a great music educator. Told
with passion and honesty in straightforward prose that feels like a
medium tempo, straight-ahead jazz tune that swings so hard and
feels so good, he reveals to us that music got inside his body at an
early age, and he was determined to share his love of the art with
the world. And no one or nothing could stop him from this life
pursuit. His primary world for many years was as a music educator
at Philadelphia's Overbrook High School, his alma mater, where he
became the first African American department head.

Along the pathways of this journey, we learn about his love of
family and his love of sports, particularly, basketball, the most

natural choice for him to play because of his tall height. You also learn that George participated in virtually every music ensemble in Philadelphia open to him as a clarinetist, primarily, including all types of bands and orchestras. You learn that his greatest love, professionally, was music—good music, like the Philadelphia Orchestra, Metropolitan Opera, and the Lincoln Center Jazz Orchestra; the great jazz musicians of Philadelphia like John Coltrane, Lee Morgan, Benny Golson, McCoy Tyner, Heath Brothers, et.al; and good jazz, period.

Life's challenges, for whatever reasons, could not stop George Allen from graduating from college and getting a doctorate in music from Temple University, or getting good jobs. He loved music teaching and loved sharing his musical knowledge with all students. He did not have to be asked to become the exemplary music educator of Philadelphia Schools, whose positive influences touched the lives of hundreds of students through the years. You don't have to ask, George Allen will do anyway.

Dr. Ted McDaniel
Professor of Music
The Ohio State University

I Was Not Asked

An African American Educator from Philadelphia Spreads His Love for Music

Dr. George E. Allen

ISBN: 978-1-4669-8353-3 (sc)
ISBN: 978-1-4669-8352-6 (hc)
ISBN: 978-1-4669-8351-9 (e)

Library of Congress Control Number: 2013903976

Trafford rev. 04/18/2013

 www.trafford.com

North America & international
toll-free: 1 888 232 4444 (USA & Canada)
phone: 250 383 6864 ♦ fax: 812 355 4082

This book is dedicated to the memory of my son,
David Henry Allen, who transitioned on March 23, 2013.

ACKNOWLEDGMENTS

This project would not have been possible without the support and cooperation of others. I want to thank Patricia Ford (Nneka) whose generous and steadfast support of this project was invaluable, and my support group "The Ambassadors." Among the important contribution to the project were interviewees, family members, music educators, and musicians. Many kept me on track and gave me the benefit of outside eyes. I appreciate all those that reminded me that the book is about students and not about me. Also, I would like to thank Ms. Clark for the four "Ds" I earned in English at West Chester Teachers College.

CONTENTS

CHAPTER ONE

On Saturday August 5, 2000, I was out walking when one of my former music students Cleveland Jenkins called out, "Hey, Mr. Allen." I had not seen Cleveland since he graduated from Overbrook High School as a music-magnet major and star basketball player about twenty-five years ago. He told me that he had gone to University of California—San Diego. He went on to play professional basketball in the NBA, traveled to Europe and South America, and was presently working with children in a sports program in Philadelphia. He told me that "music had prepared him for life." I thought on how music had played an important part in my development as a music educator, a basketball player, and a productive human being. After giving him my card, it was time for me to begin serious work on writing about my experiences as a music educator in Philadelphia because I did it differently with satisfying results.

The idea for this project began at my doctoral defense in 1997 at Temple University in Philadelphia. At the dissertation defense, one of my committee members suggested that because of the rich and diverse material in the dissertation, he thought it would be of interest to a diverse reading audience. The title of my dissertation is "The Contribution of the Philadelphia

African American Musicians to Jazz Music from 1945 to 1960."
After much introspection, I began to do taped interviews with
my sisters, cousins, and a dear friend of the family, Mrs. Fannie
Steward, who has known me through the years. The purpose of
this book is to tell about my experiences as a music educator in
the school district of Philadelphia.

I was raised and educated in Philadelphia, except for a few
early years in Lawnside, New Jersey. After traveling to many
cities across this country, I have found Philadelphia to be the
correct tempo for me, and I plan to reside here always. I was
born on December 3, 1936 (the same month that Ludwig Van
Beethoven was born back in December 1770), at the Lady of
Lourdes Hospital, which is located across the Delaware River
from Philadelphia in Camden, New Jersey. Philadelphia has
many historical sites, such as Independence Hall, the Liberty
Bell, Pennsylvania Hospital, Old Christ Church, Penn's Landing,
Walnut Theater, and the Ben Franklin Hotel. Philadelphia was
also the home of African American musician Frank Johnson.
Society Hill, located east of center city, was one of the first places
where African Americans lived as early as the seventeenth century
around Pine, Lombard, and South Streets.

Around 1936, many African Americans were moving to
Philadelphia because it was more livable than many northern
cities like Washington, DC, New York, or Boston. Philadelphia
was the "city of homes" and was affordable. The migration of
African Americans to the north, which began at about 1915, was
important for several reasons. First, a large number of individuals

were involved; second, those migrating entered a totally new environment; and last, the white population was obliged to adapt themselves to a sudden tremendous increase in a single new population of African Americans.

My grandparents migrated from Maryland and Virginia in the early 1900s in search of better living conditions for themselves. They saw economic motives as the paramount reason to migrate. Many of the male members of the Allen family were construction workers. As a young man, my father worked on the White and Black Horse Pikes in New Jersey as well as the Ben Franklin Bridge, which connects Camden and Philadelphia. He also worked on the addition to the Inquirer Building where he built the largest free-swinging scaffold at that time in Philadelphia for the John Donahue Construction Company.

Philadelphia had a large population of premigration African Americans who had developed a strong class structure. As Devlin (1985) states, "Had blacks been allowed to escape to the cotton mills in the light of severe agricultural problems, it was quite possible that fewer of them would have 'escaped' to New York, Philadelphia, and Washington." The Allen family was not a part of this group. Some migrants were better prepared than others to fit into that structure by having stronger reasons for coming as well as greater resources. Differences among migrants influenced their reception by more-established African American Philadelphians, what churches they attended, and their success in the city's emerging black neighborhoods. Philadelphia's African American population grew from 62,000 in 1900 to 134,200 in

1920. By 1940, the African American population was 118,859 according to the Sixteenth Census of the United States: 1940.

Because it was near the waterfront and center city, South Philadelphia was the first section of the city to attract migrating African Americans; it was followed at about 1940 by North Philadelphia and West Philadelphia. My family was part of the migration from South Philadelphia to West Philadelphia and was one of the early African American families to move to the 500 block of North Allison Street in 1942. My parents remained there for the remainder of their lives. These neighborhoods of African Americans did not form the ghetto as in New York's Harlem and Chicago's South Side. Philadelphia had a number of both small and large African American neighborhoods scattered throughout the city. These neighborhoods developed distinctive personalities and reputations. For example, the West Philadelphia neighborhood where I lived was divided into the "top" and the "bottom." It was divided by Fifty-Second Street from Market Street to Lansdowne Avenue: west of Fifty-Second Street was the "top," and east of Fifty-Second Street was the "bottom." You wouldn't go to the "bottom" by yourself because it was considered the rough part of town. However, as a group we would go to the Fans Theater at Fifty-First and Haverford Avenue and play basketball at the Dunlap school yard and Mill Creek Recreation Center at Forty-Eighth and Brown Street.

Philadelphia had depressed and blighted African American neighborhoods: the old court and bandbox sections of the river wards, tenement neighborhoods along the Lombard Street corridor, and the north side Tenderloin neighborhoods. Small-house neighborhoods near Girard College in North Philadelphia; above Market Street in West Philadelphia and in Germantown; home-owning neighborhoods in West Philadelphia where I lived and upper North Philadelphia; satellite suburban communities in LaMott, Chester, Darby, and Yeadon; and towns along the mainline such as Ardmore, Bryn Mawr, and Malvern were the better places to live. Many of Philadelphia's premigration African Americans lived in large, well-appointed homes in North Philadelphia on Diamond Street and Girard Avenue. They continued to live there in the '40s, '50s, and the '60s. Columbia (Cecil B. Moore) and Ridge Avenues developed into African American commercial and entertainment districts that competed with South Street in South Philadelphia.

Despite a social support system, which was basically the church, African Americans lived under the social strain in Philadelphia that was created by early industrialization. It was the major cause of racial outbreaks, political agitation, labor organizing, and general turmoil. On the other hand, affordable housing, along with the aforementioned motivational conditions, made Philadelphia unique. Because real estate, land, and rentals in Philadelphia were priced lower than in most northern cities, a high percentage of African Americans were homeowners. Expansion of the city's single-family row houses afforded a substantial proportion of its wage earners opportunities for home ownership. By 1940, the city had an exceptionally high number of African American homeowners, a startling fact considering their limited economic opportunities.

Sidebar: 12/21/1997. Johnny Coles passed on in Philadelphia.

My father, David Allen, did construction work, and my mother, Lillian Allen, was a domestic when she did work. The white migration to the "automobile suburbs" did not begin until after the Second World War. African Americans became real beneficiaries of the "city of homes," buying a relatively new house abandoned by whites. According to Hardy (1989), the single-family row house was the best thing that Philadelphia had to offer African Americans.

> Many [African Americans] migrants found that a small piece of open yard or porch made Philadelphia more livable. Southerners also brought north an inclination for home ownership, and West Philadelphia was considered "the place" to buy a home. (Hardy, 1989)

The family home in West Philadelphia was considered the place to buy homes that were bought from whites who were moving to the northeast section of Philadelphia. My parents bought such a home; it was a two-story house with three bedrooms, a living and dining room, a kitchen, and a vestibule. It also had a porch and a backyard. Most South Philadelphia houses did not have porches, but they had white marble steps, which were cleaned every Saturday morning. Cleaning the neighbors' steps was one of the ways you earned money to go to the movies.

Neighborhood transition generally took place without the firebombing, physical assaults, and tensions that scarred Chicago, New York, and Detroit. My neighborhood did not experience these conditions. As a young child, I was not aware of racism. That came later. E. Digby Baltzell, the famous University of Pennsylvania sociologist who wrote *The Philadelphia Gentlemen: The Makings of a National Upper Class* (1958), characterized Philadelphia as provincial and patrician, as compared to older Boston or newer Chicago. It was patrician because of the clannishness among affluent white families composing its social and financial institutions. Charles S. Johnston (1925) states the following characteristics about new African American urban cities.

> New York City with its "Polite service workers" and the Delightful Harlem, "the Mecca of Negroes the country Over;" Cleveland "with a faint Southern exposure but with its sophistication of skill and fancy wages;" and Philadelphia "with its comfortable old traditions." (1925)

For some African American migrants, Philadelphia was a poor choice economically, especially for those with education, skill, ambition, and vision (Heath, interview, 1994). This might partially be the reason for the drop in Philadelphia's African American population in 1940.

As stated before, I was born in Camden, but my parents were living in Lawnside, New Jersey, which is located about ten miles east of Camden, New Jersey. Lawnside is an African American community of working-class families. It was incorporated in 1926. My parents moved there at about 1934. We lived in Lawnside for about five years. The Allen family at that time consisted of my parents, me, and an older brother, David Henry Jr. We moved to the 1900 block of Watkins Street located in South Philadelphia, the same block where my mother's sister Marguerite Taylor lived. I don't remember much about my brother other than we called him Puddy. I do remember one story as told by my cousin Gloria Harris (Sissy).

During an interview with Sissy on August 20, 1999, she states the following:

> I have a story, I don't know if it has so much to do with the music development. I have a story about George which is a favorite story of mine. I don't know if it has so much to do with his showing at a young age for his thirst for knowledge.
>
> At one point in our lives my cousin George and I lived in the same block. We lived in Watkins Street, the 1900 block of Watkins Street. My aunt, George's mother, was in the hospital at the time.

Well at the time George had a brother, an older brother who we all called "Puddy." Well "Puddy" was short and stocky. George was always tall and lean. So the babysitter, I guess, didn't know their ages, obviously, she didn't know their ages. My mother had sent me down to the house, to get something, and when I went in the house, poor little "Puddy" was laid out on the floor kicking and screaming, "It's me, it's me, I'm the one, I'm the one." And George was standing over him straight and tall, all dressed up in his nice little clothes and his nice shirt and pants and everything and a little cap, standing tall and all ready to go to school. And I ran back and I told my mother and she went down to the house to straighten it out. "Puddy" was the one that went to school, George didn't go to school. But George saw his opportunity and that was the day he was going to school. We always wondered what George would have done had he been able to pull this off and go to school. So that was the beginning at a very young age for his thirst for knowledge.

I was only five years old. David was killed by a car in 1944 while playing baseball on the street.

On December 23, 1999, I interviewed my two sisters, Beatrice Lacy and Marguerite Byrd, and two cousins Gloria Harris and

Brenda Neely to give some insight of my family growing up in Philadelphia during the '40s and '50s.

Interview—Gloria's home, Philadelphia, December 23, 1999, with Gloria Harris (Sissy), Beatrice Lacy (Bea Bea), Marguerite Byrd, and Brenda Neely.

My first question to them was, where did my parents come from? They stated that they thought my mother came from Virginia because we would visit my mother's aunt Rebecca. She lived near the Rappahannock River in the northeast part of Virginia. Gloria remembers the outhouse and how dark it was at night. She also remembers being chased from the store. She believed they might have been the Klan's men. My father would drive; the trip would take about ten hours via Route 1 in a Hudson Hornet car. They all agreed that there were nine people in the car: three adults and six children. The Hudson Hornet was a big car. My father did all the driving as I would with my family on trips with six or seven children and two or three adults. However, I drove a station wagon or a van. According to Marguerite, the Hudson was black with a yellow top.

My family and cousins made trips to Atlantic City, New Jersey, and stayed at Aunt Lola's. Her house was located near Ohio Avenue, just north of Arctic Avenue. I always remember she had a windup record player. I would play the record "It Ain't Gonna Rain No More, No More." We would get the ferry to Camden and catch a train to Atlantic City. Gloria stated it was a treat to ride the train and go to the beach during the day and the boardwalk at night. Most of the group thought that the Atlantic City trips took place at the time of the Second World War. My mother's brothers participated: Uncles Russell, Ernest, Buster, and Leon. We also took trips to Coney Island, Niagara Falls, and Saint Albans, New York. When we went to Saint Albans, we would visit Aunt Marie and Uncle Charley. That was where Count Basie and Jackie Robinson lived.

Aunt Lola would tell us stories about my mother and aunt. My sister Bea Bea remembered the following story as told by Aunt Lola.

> They like to go to parties and she said that they would go to dances and she said they would use lard on their hair to make it lay down. Sometimes they would get home late because my mother liked to get the last dance. (Interview, December 23, 1999)

Gloria thought of my mother as being meek and mild. Her mother was the more aggressive and adventurous one of the two. She also thought my mother was the youngest. In reality, my aunt was the more adventurous of the two. After my father passed in 1975, my mother and aunt traveled all over the world with family friends Ms. Harriett and Aunt Una.

I asked the group their impressions of me as a young musician. Beatrice stated, "All three of us took music lessons, but I was the only one who did something with it." Gloria went on to say, "Music was just something that everybody seemed to do, take piano lessons." She continues,

> And saw George as having been picked by your father to do this. And I don't think that you were a rebellious child, so you never to me seemed to cause any rebellion against studying or playing . . . . Ah, but I always saw your father as the motivator, the aggressive one to keep you going this direction. (Interview, December 23, 1999)

Beatrice added, "He was destined . . . it was part of his destination." Gloria and Brenda's brother, Elwood Taylor, had a strong influence on developing my interest in the arts. He was an impeccable dresser and had a wonderful record collection of jazz and classical music. He also played the guitar and trumpet. I influenced Elwood to attend Cheyney University. He became an English teacher in the Philadelphia School District.

When the families moved to West Philadelphia, Brenda said that we became more cultural minded. She continues that we walked different and we talked different. We sort of sat up straight and walked a little more dignified. You didn't slouch; you didn't stroll. It wasn't a West Philadelphia thing. It was a South Philadelphia thing. Marguerite and Brenda stated they experienced territorial kinds of cultural differences based on skin color and economics. Based on these differences, you might not be invited to a party in Germantown or Yeadon. I did not have this situation because I played music and basketball. All of them stated that they spent most of their time with friends in the neighborhood. At the end of the interview, they all agreed that they did not expect me to get married and have all those babies. We raised thirteen children, six of ours and seven grandchildren.

CHAPTER TWO

I attended Brooks Elementary School from 1942 to 1948. The school was located at Fifty-Seventh and Haverford Avenue. The school was named after George Brooks, who came to Philadelphia from Holmfirth, Yorkshire, England, in 1859. He had an upholstering business named the Oriental Mills and built some of the first stone-front houses on the 500 block of Fifty-Fifth Street with stones from the Centennial Exposition. His son, Henry, sold to the school district land to build Brooks School for the sum of $12,000 in 1901. The school was built in 1902 but was destroyed by fire on January 23, 1918. The school was rebuilt in 1919 with twenty-one classrooms and a manual training classroom. Henry Brooks was active in government as a councilman of the thirty-fourth ward and clerk of the Quarter Sessions Court. George Brooks Elementary School was closed in 1972.

The faculty at Brooks School during the time I attended was Mr. Blumberg, principal; and Mrs. Brown, secretary. The teachers were Dannehauer, Duckett, Fauset, Fogarty, Pastore, Viseidy, Mueller, Thompson, Clark, and Mr. DiToro. The African American teachers were Clark, Duckett, Faucet, and Thompson, and I believe they all lived within walking distance from the school. Brooks Elementary School was a typical elementary school in Philadelphia at the time. We had white students who lived around Fifty-Seventh and Vine Street, and the school went from kindergarten to sixth grade.

My kindergarten teacher was Ms. Thompson, who lived in the neighborhood. I know because I would watch her walk to and from school. It was in kindergarten that I met my wife, Gladys Eloise Peters. She was the brightest student in the class; she knew how to read. When asked, she would read stories to the class that Ms. Thompson would ask her to read. Before nap time, we would have milk and graham crackers. One day, Eloise noticed that I was not drinking my milk. She asked why I was not drinking my milk. I said, "I don't like white milk." She exchanged my white milk for her chocolate milk. This began a sixty-year relationship. We were married for forty-three years.

Brooks Elementary school was a musical school. Many of the teachers played the piano very well like Ms. Thompson, Ms. Muller, and the school secretary, Ms. Brown. Ms. Muller led the school choir and assembly. Eloise played the piano and was a vocal soloist with the school choir. The choir was excellent. I think I was in the choir because I could read music, but I did not have a "solo"-quality voice. The choir sang for the school in concerts, in school plays, and in the community. We sang two- and three-part vocal literatures. For assembly, all students sang from yellow or blue songbooks. Those songs were not taught by rote. The *Blue Book of Songs* had songs by the great European composers: Bach, Beethoven, and Brahms. I remember one song in particular, the "Anvil Chorus" from *Aida* by Verdi. The *Yellow*

Book of Songs had patriotic songs. Also, all my classroom teachers taught music to their classes. Music and art were a part of the curriculum in the lower grades. I do not remember music taught by my fifth-and sixth-grade teachers, but I remember we did make presentations for assembly programs that included music and public speaking. I remember my sixth grade class performing "The Creation" by James Weldon Johnson.

Many students at Brooks went on to prominence, the most famous being Wilt Chamberlain, who became one of the most famous NBA basketball players. Chamberlain died on October 12, 1999, of heart failure in Los Angeles. He was sixty-four years old. Others were Willie Williams, past commissioner of police; Jackie Moore, the first African American to play for the Philadelphia Warriors professional basketball team; Dr. Jeanette Brewer, James "Blinky" Brown, and Karin Helene Bivins—school district administrators; and Rose Montgomery and Patricia Tildon—music educators.

My favorite teacher was Mr. DiToro, my sixth grade teacher. He had a wonderful mind; he seemed to know everything. When any questions came up in assembly and the other teachers didn't know the answer, he did. He was also a disciplined person, and so were his classes. Mr. DiToro had an air of authority like our principal, Mr. Blumberg. I was not the best-disciplined student. Ms. Fossett, my fourth grade teacher, had the reputation as the sternest teacher in the school and the community. Everybody knew Ms. Fossett. So we knew from the first day who was in charge. I made an effort to behave all year until the last day. I had earned an S in cooperation for the year: one hundred and eighty days! On the last day, I decided it was OK to do my thing. I don't know what I did, but I do know she took me to the dressing room and gave my artistic hands a workout with the fifteen-inch ruler. I must say that I learned more in fourth and sixth grades than any other grades at Brooks Elementary School. Ms. Fossett and Mr. DiToro were wonderful and dedicated teachers. The biggest talk among the girls was the notes passed between Ms. Pastore, Ms. Viscidy, and Mr. DiToro. Mr. DiToro married Ms. Viscidy.

I began my formal music lessons soon after I started school. My first music teacher was Mr. C. Wyatt Graves, who had a music studio in his home in the 400 block of Fifty-Fifth Street near Haverford Avenue. I don't know where he received his training, but I'm positive he was not self-taught. Mr. Graves taught all the instruments. This may have started my interest in becoming a music teacher. I took piano lessons first and then some clarinet lessons. It was in the fourth grade where I met Mr. Chance, my first public school instrumental teacher. I was selected to play the clarinet, which became my primary instrument. Mr. Chance taught the basics of playing the clarinet. I learned very quickly. I went though book one of the Rubank clarinet method in six months. Taking piano lessons from Mr. Graves was a great help. I still recommend to parents that the piano should be the first instrument a child plays. It is so basic. I was lucky. Mr. Graves started me on the Thompson piano method. I think I went through five or six books. At this point,

I would like to mention that Mr. Graves was the only African American music teacher I encountered from elementary to my DMA from Temple University, which I earned in 1997. In fact, I don't remember having any African American teachers after elementary school. I wonder how many African Americans can make that statement of fact.

In the eighth grade, Mr. Chance was a positive influence in my making an early decision to become a music educator. That is when the choice would be whether one was going to take academic, commercial, or industrial courses in high school. Unfortunately, in many cases, this was decided for many African Americans. If you had a discipline problem or average grades, you were put in industrial or commercial; if not, you might be placed in the academic course. I was fortunate. I'll also talk about this later. Mr. Chance received his degree from the University of Pennsylvania. His major instrument was the organ. During the summer, the School District of Philadelphia had a music program in collaboration with the Philadelphia Department of Recreation. I continued my clarinet lessons during the summer and played in the small instrumental ensembles in the mornings. I participated in the recreation program in the afternoons. This was the period in my life that I developed my interest in sports. I don't remember any students from this group continuing in music as a profession. I can't remember a time when I did not play music after I moved to West Philadelphia. It seemed as though there was always a piano in the left-hand corner of the living room.

We had one of the better homes on the block because my father was handy at repairs and remodeling. He learned this from doing construction work all his life. He had a sixth grade education. Mother had a high school diploma. I didn't have many chores around the house when I was in elementary school, even less when I went to junior and senior high school. I think my mother and father believed I was going to become the next Duke Ellington. Duke Ellington's mother treated him like a prince. I often heard my peers talking about what they had to do around the house when they were growing up. I didn't do many of these things, like washing or ironing clothes, cleaning my room, or cleaning the front of the house. The only thing I had to do was put out the ashes and garbage. The other chores were left to my sisters, Beatrice and Marguerite. Some husbands and fathers managed the art of cooking through the years in case they are called to do so in an emergency. Not me. My one and only cooking experience ended with my mother-in-law coming through the front door, announcing to my kids, "Don't eat it." She had stopped by for a visit. I had prepared something that was not too fresh. This was while I was home alone with the kids. In other words, I'm a disaster in the kitchen.

Sidebar: 5/24/2001. Listened to Beethoven's Appassionata Sonata, Op. 78, today on the radio.

The neighborhood streets served a dual purpose—as transportation routes for the disappearing horse and wagon, making way for automobiles and trolley cars, and as playgrounds for games. The street games I played were pimple ball, awning ball, handball, dead box played with bottle caps, wall ball, and touch football. A foul ball to the stomach ended my interest in playing baseball. During this time, baseball was more popular than basketball in the African American community.

CHAPTER THREE

After graduating from George Brooks Elementary School, I went to Shoemaker Junior High School for three years. The music teachers were Ms. Treille and Mr. Chance. Ms. Treille was the general music teacher, and Mr. Chance was the instrumental teacher. Mr. Chance had a room across the hall from the auditorium and a rehearsal room on the fourth floor. That is where I spent many hours practicing, being excused from general music classes and more than a few academic classes. I earned average grades in my academic subjects. This decision not to go to class proved problematic in eighth grade when it became time to choose a course for high school.

Sidebar: 7/19/2001. Listened the Mozart's Clarinet Concerto in A Major, K 622. Emma Johnson, soloist on the radio.

When it came time to choose a course, I chose academic music. My counselor said I was not academic material because my grades were average. I was signed up for the industrial course that prepared students for jobs in industry. One took shop classes along with low-level academic classes. This was the pattern for many African Americans: industrial for boys and commercial for girls who had average scores or grades or some kind of discipline problem. I had some discipline problems because academic classes were boring for me. No one ever explained to me the purpose of writing a word five times and using the word in a sentence. I think I would have learned more if I was homeschooled, but that was not an alternative. So I would act up in class.

I had average grades and excellent attendance. I can't say that I did not like school. For the most part, teachers did not give the individual attention like my music teachers: Mr. Graves, Mr. Chance, and clarinet teacher Mr. Liberio. I was focused on music and basketball. Thank goodness my father was focused on my ambition to be a music educator. He met with my counselor and demanded that I be placed in the academic course. I was not asked. My father was the real motivation for me pursuing music. He told friends while working in Ocean City, New Jersey, as a young man that if he had a son, he would want him to play music. I was that son. He was my moral and financial support. One of the people my father told this was Mrs. Fannie Steward. I interviewed Mrs. Fannie Steward on June 26, 1999.

Before answering interview questions, Aunt Fannie talked about being raised in Virginia, her mother (a teacher), and her father (a minister). Aunt Fannie was married to Paul Steward, who met my father in Ocean City where they were working on building the boardwalk. They became lifelong friends. She stated that my father would bring me to her house on Sundays to play for them pieces I had learned that week. I have always enjoyed playing for people and performing in front of a class of students or performing groups.

I remember a trip I took to Virginia with Aunt Fannie and her husband. One day, I was over at their house and wanted to know why they were packing. They were going to Aunt Fannie's uncle's farm in Nottaway County, Virginia. I asked, "Could I go?" They said, "Ask your parents." Of course they said yes. I was impressed with Aunt Fannie's uncle because he would carry a shotgun because there were snakes in the fields where we picked vegetables. She stated that I kept asking him to shoot the gun. When we were ready to return to the house, he turned the gun up in the air and fired it. Aunt Fannie said that I shouted, "Please, no more. Don't shoot it no more. I've had enough." I was not asked. I don't remember ever holding or shooting a gun and have never had one in the house.

Aunt Fannie became an unofficial advisor to my family, particularly my father, who had some problems with me growing up—practically with school. I had some disciplinary problems because, as stated before, the academics were boring for me. Aunt Fannie was very intelligent. She has helped me out of situations I got myself into with the school district. She retired from the school district as a home and school coordinator supervisor. My wife worked under her supervision. Her office was at Overbrook High where I became the department head of the Fine Arts Magnet Program. She was my eyes and ears. I was the only African American department head. I did a little better academically in ninth grade because I had a strong homeroom teacher by the name of Ms. Bowers and a supportive homeroom class. There were two academic ninth grade sections (9A1 and 9A2). I was in the top section, which I believed was tracked. Matthew Robinson from Sesame Street and Ira Davis, who went to the 1958 and 1962 Olympics, were in this class. The school year was divided into A and B terms, and there were two graduations per school year.

Many of my classmates were about the academics. They would help me catch up with back assignments, especially Latin and English, which have always been difficult for me. They also let me practice for my private clarinet lessons in the classroom, which I took after school on Fridays with Mr. Anthony Liberio. At about the sixth grade, I began to study privately with Mr. Liberio at the Knects Music Store, located in the 100 block of south Eighteenth Street. I studied with Mr. Liberio for about fifteen years. He had the greatest influence on me as a musician. In the fifteen years of studying with him, he only played for me twice; one time, he played the clarinet solo from the "Mozartina" by Peter Ilich Tchaikovsky to demonstrate the use of the left hand. The second time, he played the clarinet solo from the Symphony no. 6 in B Minor, Op. 72, Pathetique, by Tchaikovsky to demonstrate how a clarinet should sound. I was not asked. At the time, I was fascinated by fast notes. Musicianship is important. In order to become an effective music educator, one must be a fine musician, which I'm told I have achieved.

Sidebar: 7/23/2001. Tchaikovsky's Piano Concerto no. 1 in B Flat Minor, Op. 23, is playing on the radio.

I was first chair in All-Junior High Orchestra, All-Senior High Orchestra and Band, Philadelphia Youth Orchestra, All-State Band, West Chester States Teachers College, State Collegiate Band, and Philadelphia Symphony Club Orchestra and Band.

The Philadelphia District had a Saturday morning program at the old high school for girls located at 1700 Spring Garden Streets. Group lessons were given, and there was an All-City Junior High Orchestra. With a recommendation from your home school music teacher, you could audition. I passed and became a member of the orchestra in 1948. For the first time, I was a member of a predominately white music group. This pattern would continue for most of my career as a musician and music educator.

Every year at Shoemaker, there was a talent show that gave first, second, and third prizes. I played in seventh and eighth grade but never won first prize. Playing classical music didn't help when the judges were your peers. In ninth grade, I was approached by two classmates and neighborhood friends—Harry Caldwell, who lived on the 500 block of Vodges Street, the next block from my block; and James Lee, who lived on the 1400 block of Fifty-Seventh Street—with the idea of forming a jazz band. Reluctant at first, we started rehearsing at Harry's house after school. Harry played piano, James played clarinet, and

I played alto saxophone, which I began playing along with the clarinet and piano. Harry and James didn't read music. We were not playing Byrd or Miles. It was a jazz piece that was popular on the radio at the time. Harry had a fine ear for music. He showed me what to play. I showed James. I don't remember the name of the piece, but Harry told me what to do. My instructions were to play loud and find something slick to wear at the talent show. That Friday afternoon, we became certified stars by our peers. It was amazing to me because to think I only had to play four or five notes. They must have been the correct ones.

PICTURE
Talent show, June 1951 at Shoemaker Junior High

The Shoemaker Cobbler (1951)

I wish that I would have taken improvisation seriously. In junior high, I changed piano teachers. Mr. Dellrigio gave me private lessons at home. Along with the normal piano repertoire, he also introduced me to some jazz styles from a piano book. I played what was on the page. I didn't swing at all. I didn't get an opportunity to improvise at the lessons but did some trial and error on my own, but it didn't have any form. Now, when I have an opportunity to practice, I spend part of the time creating and improvising etudes and compositions. It makes practicing more interesting. For budding musicians, one should just start playing what you hear in your head. Don't worry, the more you do it, the better it gets, and you will gain your confidence. Improvising is like speaking; you think of words before you speak them. Reading music should be like reading words; the music should sing back to you. Later on in my career, I discovered Dr. Edwin Gordon's music learning theory. In retrospect, I'm surprised that I did not do more because I found basketball to be a game of improvisation for me. I could have used the same in learning music. According to my peers, I was very creative on the basketball court. Classical music just took up most of my time. Jazz music was relaxing for me.

On graduation day, I was suspended from school. I don't remember what I did, but it was something crazy like not being where I was supposed to be. The only reason I participated in graduation was because I was on the program to play a solo. Mr. Chance and music saved me. To this day, I still refuse to grow up. To me, it seems better to look at life though a child's eye. In other words, I intend to stay young at heart. I do have a serious side, but the "child's eye" seems to be present in the background. In other words, I don't take life too serious. I heard Kenny Baron, jazz pianist, say this at a Temple University workshop.

Sidebar: On the *Today* morning show, there was an African American woman celebrating her 119th birthday. She wanted a man and some Royal Crown Whiskey for her birthday.

CHAPTER FOUR

In September 1951, I enrolled at Overbrook High School, located at Fifty-Ninth and Lancaster Avenue in West Philadelphia, in the academic-music course. Overbrook opened in 1926 with three thousand students who were predominantly Caucasian and Jewish. The two music teachers were Mr. Louis Krass, orchestra and theory/harmony, and Mr. Henry Loper, band and choir. Mr. Loper was also the conductor of the 12B senior class choir to learn graduation music. We sounded and looked great. This was no surprise because we had sung since first grade.

Overbrook had a fine reputation for music, academics, basketball, and track. The academic-music course consisted of the normal academic subjects. There was one period of theory and practice in the tenth grade and harmony in the eleventh and twelfth grades. Orchestra practiced during the school day, and band practiced before and after school. The curriculum was for those students who wished to prepare for entrance to schools or colleges specializing in the field of music. I didn't do much better with the academes because I was competing with Jewish students from Beeber Junior High. They were prepared for high school. Beeber is located at Fifty-Ninth and Malvern in the Wynnefield section of West Philadelphia. Jewish students also came from the Parkside section of West Philadelphia, which bordered Fairmont Park. Fairmont Park is the largest park located within a city; it is larger than Central Park in New York City.

I remember wondering why they could read the Latin translations like they were reading English. So one day in band, I asked Paul Munin, who sat next to me, how come they translated the Latin so well. He said, "We use the pony." This was a book that had the translations. I did not know about the "pony." He told me that I could buy it at Leary's Book Store. After sharing this information with my peers, the next day, I was at the bookstore. Because of that, brothers and sisters learned about Caesar and the Gaul Wars. Students from Shoemaker didn't have an option to study French or Spanish because these were not offered.

Paul and I became good friends. His family owned a trophy store in center city. We would walk over the Fifty-Fifth Street Bridge to his house in Wynnefield to practice and play duets. He later studied with my clarinet teacher, Mr. Liberio. Paul lived in Wynnefield, which had large single homes near Fairmont Park east and west of Fifty-Fourth Street. Many African Americans did day work in Wynnefield. Overbrook was a good school for African Americans who had college as a goal. It was good for those who had gotten over the academic stereotypes at the time. "You are not academic material." According to Leroy Layton, former principal at Overbrook, "Many Overbrook graduates went on to earn advanced degrees." West Philadelphia High

School, located at Forty-Seventh and Walnut Street, was another good school for African Americans. I did learn because of the environment in spite of a lack of good study habits.

Overbrook is located at one of the highest elevations in the city. Overbrook students are called hill-toppers. The mascot is the panther. The school colors are orange and black. Students from my neighborhood walked up Fifty-Seventh or Forty-Ninth Street in the warm weather and rode the "G" bus in the winter. Some mornings, we would get to school about an hour before advisory to complete assignments or go to before-school activities. With so much going on with music and basketball, there wasn't much time for homework. I was also playing in two independent basketball leagues.

The normal day for me after school was rehearsal, practice, and basketball. Saturday, it was clarinet lessons, basketball, lunch, and listening to the Metropolitan Opera. Later, I would take my mother shopping on Ninth Street in South Philadelphia. In the evening, I would dress and go to the Philadelphia Orchestra concert. Then I would then meet my cousin Elwood Taylor at Board and South to listen to jazz. He would sneak me into the clubs because I was underage. I was sixteen. The bouncers at Peps and Showboat started letting me in because they knew I was studying music and interested in jazz. I didn't have time to go to the movies on Saturdays; I was too involved in the music and basketball.

I have been busy all my life: maybe not doing all things at the right time and place. Many things can be learned just by movement and curiosity. For example, last summer I became curious about Gustav Mahler's Symphonies. I brought the scores to all the symphonies and the Deutsche Grammophon (stereo 435162-2) box set with Leonard Bernstein conducting. I did an informal analysis. My observations are twofold: first, how could one human being write so many notes; and second, conducting the slow movements would be a problem for me because my heart could not beat that slow. Mahler is trying to move into first place as one of my favorite composers. Right now, Beethoven is still the favorite, but Johann Sebastian Bach is in charge of music in heaven and would argue also for jazz.

There is a strong relationship between the two styles. I would also argue that in order to perform jazz, one should study European classical music first. The days of the Louis Armstrongs and Earl Gardners have passed. They did not have the opportunity to study formally. You must study European classical music; Wynton Marsalis has led the path. There are many more opportunities to study music today. Because of my interest in jazz and Philadelphia, the following is from my dissertation: "Contributions of the Philadelphia African American Musicians to American Jazz Music from 1945 to 1960."

The migration of African Americans to the North, in Philadelphia in particular, had a direct impact upon the evolution of jazz. In learning jazz, jazz musicians pass through common developmental stages. According to Fraser (1984), there are five developmental stages: (1) attraction to jazz music, (2) ear training and observation, (3) manipulation of an instrument, (4) emulation of models and refinement, and (5) self-actualization and individual stylistic development (p. 30).

From 1945 to 1960, Philadelphia's Black Musician's Local 274 provided African American musicians with many opportunities to cultivate these five developmental stages. Many Philadelphia African American jazz musicians attributed their success to the atmosphere and fellowship at Black Local 274. For aspiring musicians, the Local was a training ground for developing their reputation and experimenting with new musical concepts. Local 274 was also a place where African American musicians sought refuge from racial prejudice and discrimination. In the union club during the jam sessions, musicians were encouraged to pursue musical careers through the applause of grassroots Philadelphia African Americans who loved and respected them and the visiting jazz musicians who were playing in the local clubs (Turner 1993, 204). Many members of Local 274 joined because of these benefits (Coles 1995; Simms 1995; Heath, P., 1994). The atmosphere inspired both African American and white musicians. They learned by listening to the music performed at the Union and socializing with the many musicians who congregated there.

> The fellowship, exchange of musical ideas and preservation of a black cultural identity became primary attractions for white musicians who later joined Local 274. (Turner 1993, 170)

Local 274 prospered because many of its members, such as John Coltrane, Benny Golson, Lee Morgan, and the Heath Brothers, gained national prominence as jazz musicians. These musicians moved on to New York, but they never forgot their affiliations in Philadelphia. By the end of the 1950s, Local 274 had nine hundred members (Turner 1993, 206). Simms (1995) and Turner (1993) have called Philadelphia a Cradle of Jazz, and Jimmy Heath, in an interview with Porter (1995), stated that Philadelphia was known as a city of "second-line beboppers."

Many African American jazz musicians refined their playing and developed their styles in Philadelphia venues. Jazz clubs throughout the city provided young musicians opportunities for exposure: the Showboat and Pep's Musical Bar in South Philadelphia, the Blue Note Club in North Philadelphia, and the 421 Club and the Harlem Club in West Philadelphia (Ballard 1995; Coles 1995; Simms 1995). During the 1940s and 1950s, Saturday matinees from 2:00 p.m. to 6:00 p.m. were reserved to give serious young musicians opportunities to perform with established local and visiting artists. These were sometimes referred to as jam sessions.

Jam sessions were popular in Philadelphia during the mid-1940s and throughout the 1950s. Philadelphia musicians used them to learn and to forge connections with other musicians (Turner 1993, 170). They experimented with new ideas, exhibited their musical and technical skills, and competed with each other. Because musicians were judged by their peers, they were inspired to practice long hours prior to the jam sessions. J. R.

Mitchell, a Philadelphia musician and educator, had the following to say about jam sessions and the Zanzibar Club in North Philadelphia:

> Watt's [Zanzibar] became known as the "Bebop" room of Philly, and was the favorite hangout of most Philadelphia musicians who later attained fame—Coltrane, the Heath Brothers [Percy, Jimmy, and Albert], Philly Joe Jones, and Benny Golson, to name a few. At any given time, it was possible to walk into the Zanzibar and find the houseful [*sic*] of "Jazz" greats. When the bands came to the Earle Theater, or were playing anywhere in or near Philly, after the gig they would head for the Zanzibar. Every night was a continuous "Jam Session" . . . It was common to see white student musicians ruining their eyes trying to write what could be discerned by the dim lights. The Saturday afternoon matinee started at four o'clock, but if you were not in the Zanzibar at two, you were out of luck. (Turner 1993, 172)

All the aforementioned venues were places where the Philadelphia African American musicians could perfect their skills and develop new ideas before they migrated to New York or stayed in Philadelphia to develop a career.

Despite their preparation, Philadelphia African American musicians had to contend with racism, a major obstacle that sometimes led to their displacement by white musicians who had learned to play black styles of music. A *Philadelphia Tribune* article dated December 26, 1940, titled "Are Negro Bands Really on the Way off Big Time?" stated that during the 1940s, Negro orchestras suffered their greatest hardships. There were several reasons.

> First of all, white bands have more and more become adept at the musical styles which made Negroes so unique. Through the use of colored arrangers who gave that special sepia twang, careful and detailed study of the Negro's style of playing, the white musician has made himself just as good (or in some cases better) than the ordinary good Negro band. Thus, the student has surpassed the master. (Turner 1993, 137)

Philadelphia's African American musicians who received recognition in the music industry struggled against great odds. Despite hard times, the popularity of jazz made jobs available for musicians. The African American community supported jazz by their patronage of clubs, dances, and other social affairs. Premigration African Americans sponsored teas, concerts, and social affairs. Philadelphia's African American musicians who moved back and forth between New York and Philadelphia contacted the best musicians in Philadelphia when openings occurred and recommended them (Turner 1993, 173).

Philadelphia African Americans, having a reputation for being serious musicians (Primack 1979, 16), were engaged frequently to perform as traveling musicians. Opportunities to travel gave Philadelphia African American musicians access to short-term and, if fortunate, long-term engagements with outstanding groups, including the Art Blakley, John Coltrane, Miles Davis, and Dizzy Gillespie groups.

Prior to 1960, dance and jazz had always been an important part of the musical culture of African Americans. Traditionally, there is no real distinction between music and dance in African cultures (New 1983, 25). Cabaret night clubs, an important venue for jazz music and dance, disappeared in Philadelphia during the early 1960s and were not replaced with a venue providing the black communities with a similar level of community expression (Hazzard-Gordon 1990, 158).

Traveling African American musicians commonly joined Philadelphia's Black Musicians' Local 274 because it afforded musicians an opportunity to acquire a union card before going to New York. To preserve jobs for local units and eliminate competition, union officials of Local 274 made it difficult for traveling bands to acquire union cards as a group (Turner 1993, 117). Many black traveling bands disbanded so members could get their union cards. Jimmy Adams, former Local 274 president, talks about this process.

Actually, Philadelphia was known as a graveyard for bands. If an organized band came here, it broke up here . . . Any number of bands came here and broke up because of the attitudes of the union officials at the time . . . If you broke up and stayed here, okay. Everybody could work, but not as an organized band. (Turner 1993, 108)

Music education has a long-honored place in the cultures of both Philadelphia's African American and white populations. For African Americans, a music education was a combination of European and African traditions. Traditionally, European training is based on conservatory pedagogies. The focus is on developing skills required to interpret music from the written tradition. African training is based on oral transmission, and the focus is on providing functional music. For Philadelphia African American musicians, the purpose of a music education was to enable them to develop the technical proficiency required to perform written marching and dance band repertory (Ballard 1995; Coles 1995; Heath, A., 1995; Wilkinson 1994, 27).

Kwabena Nketia (1973) states that the principles of music education have been that of "slow absorption" through exposure to musical situations and active participation rather than formal teaching (p. 16). Many Philadelphia African American jazz musicians state that they were basically self-taught with some informal training from fellow musicians (Coles 1995; Heath, A., 1995; Simms 1995; Heath, P., 1994). Philadelphia jazz musicians in their early development would gather at other musicians' homes to listen to and study recordings and to practice. The Heath home was one of these homes (Coles 1995; Primack 1979, 16).

According to Franklin (1979), early public education available to Philadelphia African Americans was generally inferior to that of whites because the white majority in the city held certain beliefs and attitudes about the inferior character and capacities of African Americans; public schooling reflected these beliefs (p. xvii). I overheard one music director say, "Black students from black southern music schools in the south could only march and play marches." Changes came slowly.

> In examining the politics of African-American public schooling in Philadelphia between 1900 and 1950, the most significant changes took place during the thirties: 1) the appointment of a representative of the African-American minority to the school board, 2) the merging of the dual eligibility lists for appointments to the public elementary schools, and 3) the decision to allow African-Americans to compete for positions in the public secondary schools. (Franklin 1979, 188)

These changes were inextricably tied to larger social, political, and economic changes: (1) city improvements in race relations, (2) increases in black political power, and (3) the economic depressions. For those Philadelphia African American musicians who had the opportunity to receive music instruction in public school, the instruction was beneficial (Heath, P., 1994; Ballard 1995; Coles 1995).

Gospel music provided Philadelphia African American musicians with a source of musical concepts for individual stylistic development. During the 1950s, Philadelphia was a center for gospel music, and gospel music in turn influenced the Philadelphia jazz musicians' style (Simms 1995).

> The close relationship of jazz and religious music is demonstrated by the ease with which contemporary performers move from one area of music to the other . . . an imposing array of Negro artists in the popular field received their basic musical training in religious music and were performers in church choirs or smaller singing groups prior to entering the jazz field. (Rick 1960, 140)

Rev. Charles A. Tindley, renowned after World War I as the eloquent minister of the Tindley Temple United Methodist Church located in South Philadelphia, was the first African American to compose and publish gospel music (Jackson 1995, 190; Reagon 1992, 14). According to Ballard (1984), Thomas A. Dorsey, who is frequently identified as the father of gospel music, said that Rev. Charles A. Tindley holds this place (p. 228).

Ballard (1984) states that Philadelphia's great contribution to the development of black music is gospel music, for the city was its birthplace (p. 225).

By the 1950s, centers of gospel music performance had been established in such cities as Chicago, Detroit, New York, and Birmingham. According to Ballard (1984), gospel music symbolized the merging of the Old Philadelphia tradition with the Southern tradition (p. 225). Philadelphia African American culture contributed a strong gospel influence to jazz music by way of the churches and later through the recording industry (Reagon 1992, 22). One of the most famous of all Philadelphia gospel groups was the Ward Singers. The group included Gertrude Ward, Willa Ward Moultrie, mother, and Clara Ward, who became the most famous of the group. The Ward Singers were an internationally renowned female gospel group during the 1950s and the 1960s (Broughton 1985, 76).

During the fifties, American jazz music began to change from a commercial form to an art form (Cole 1976, 19). Jazz was becoming validated, and Philadelphia participated in the validation of this art form.

Developments in jazz in the early 1940s can be viewed as reactions to the big swing bands and the pressures on such bands to cater to public and commercial taste. The development of a concert culture for jazz meant a broadening of its base of patronage; but just as in the development of a concert culture in art-music a century or more earlier, one result was a growing lag between the musical thought of the advanced performer [jazz musician] and his public. (Hitchcock 1974, 217)

The contributions of the Philadelphia African American jazz musicians have been both quantitatively and qualitatively important to the development of African American classical music. Philadelphia was one of the cities that nurtured bebop (Heath, J., Porter, interview, 1995). Philadelphia provided education, socialization, and venues for African American jazz musicians to cultivate the five developmental stages and then move on to New York to gain recognition. Philadelphia musicians characterized the jazz community in Philadelphia as "family" (Coles 1995; Heath, J., Porter, interview, 1995; Simms 1995).

Noted Philadelphia African American jazz musicians (1945-1960): John Coltrane, Jimmy Heath, Benny Golson, and Lee Morgan.

John Coltrane

John Coltrane (b. Hamlet, North Carolina, September 23, 1926; d. New York, New York, July 17, 1967) developed his personal musical voice in Philadelphia on the way to establishing himself as one of the important innovators in jazz music (Kernfeld 1982; White III 1981; Cole 1976; Simpkins 1975).

Coltrane came to Philadelphia from High Point, North Carolina, in 1944 (Cole 1976, 25) and studied at the Ornstein School of Music and Granoff Studios located in central Philadelphia. Philadelphia proved to be ideal for Coltrane's development because he was a quiet person and apprehensive of New York's fast lifestyle (Welch 1971, 20). Coltrane found Philadelphia musicians had outstanding theoretical and instrumental skills, particularly Jimmy Heath (b. Philadelphia, October 25, 1926).

> I had met Jimmy Heath, who besides being a wonderful saxophonist, understood a lot about musical construction. (Coltrane 1960, 26)

John Coltrane and Jimmy Heath had similar musical interests. Like many jazz musicians, Coltrane and Heath transcribed or memorized recorded solos. Unlike others, both of them also used recordings to learn about writing techniques used by composers and arrangers (Cole 1976, 25-26). Coltrane also learned from Calvin Massey (b. Philadelphia, January 11, 1927; d. New York, October 25, 1972), a composer and trumpeter.

> Another friend [Calvin Massey] and I learned together in Philly . . . . His musical ideas and mine often ran parallel, and we've collaborated quite often. We helped each other advance musically by exchanging knowledge and ideas. (Coltrane 1960, 26)

During the 1940s, Coltrane worked with singer and saxophonist Eddie "Cleanhead" Vinson's rhythm and blues band and with Dizzy Gillespie's combo. In the early 1950s, Coltrane worked with the Earl Bostic and Johnny Hodges bands (Ramsey 1989, 56) and in 1952 began his relationship with Miles Davis. Crow (1990) states the following in *Jazz Anecdotes*:

> Of the many musicians Miles did hire, John Coltrane left the strongest personal stamp on his music. (p. 324)

In 1959, Coltrane recorded two noteworthy albums: (1) Miles Davis' *Kind of Blue*, recorded on March 2, 1959, in which chord changes were reduced to a bare minimum and improvisation is based on modal scales, and (2) *Giant Steps*, recorded on July 1, 1959. *Giant Steps* has one of the most demanding chord progressions in jazz.

> Looking back, I [Zwerin] suppose bebop's terminal coma began with Coltrane's *Giant Steps*, which took chord changes to their ultimate complexity, after which there was no place else to go inside that structure. (Zwerin 1983, 172-73)

Coltrane was trying for a sweeping sound that included his "sheets of sound" technique, a term coined by jazz critic Ira Gitler (Cummings 1975).

> I [Coltrane] could stack up chords—say, on a C7,
> I sometimes superimposed an Eb7, up to an F#7,
> down to an F. That way I could play three chords
> on one. (Coltrane 1960, 27)

With these two recordings, Coltrane influenced an entire new generation of saxophonists. His influence was so powerful that it also affected the styles of countless established saxophonists (Ramsey 1989, 56).

> There is hardly a saxophonist in the late 20th
> century whose playing does not reflect the
> influence of Coltrane's sound and an awareness, at
> least, of his typical melodic formulas. Such players
> include Bob Berg, Mike Brecker [Philadelphian],
> George Coleman, Dave Liebman, Joe Farrell,
> Sonny Fortune [Philadelphian], Steve Grossman,
> Charles Lloyd, and Branford Marsalis. (Kernfeld
> 1988, 1:422)

Nearly all the technically fast reed soloists heard today owe a debt to Coltrane's genius (Levey 1983, 88). Free-jazz tenor saxophonists derive their style from Coltrane, two examples being Pharoah Sanders (Farrell) of Little Rock, Arizona, and Archie Shepp of Fort Lauderdale, Florida. Archie Shepp was raised in the Germantown section of Philadelphia.

One of the most striking aspects of Coltrane's playing was his incredibly human sound (Ramsey 1989, 57). Coltrane's sound had a biting quality and a fierce emotional cry. He liberally employed overblowing, the high register, and multiphonics (Kernfeld 1988, 1:422). John Glenn, a baritone saxophone player from Philadelphia, showed Coltrane how to make two or three notes at one time (multiphonics) on tenor (Heath, J., Porter, interview, 1995). Coltrane states that it is achieved by false fingering and adjusting your lip (Cole 1976, 129).

Coltrane assimilated a wide range of Philadelphia musical influences to create the most influential personal sound and style of his time.

> He [Coltrane] had a background not only of spirituals and musical religious frenzy, but a more recent history of honking rhythm and blues, often while walking the bartops of Philly. He played with Big Maybell, 3 Bips and Bop, and later Jimmy Smith and the Dizzy Gillespie big band. (Baraka, Amiri, and Amina 1987, 300)

In 1959, when he was not performing with the Miles Davis sextet, Coltrane began experimenting with different personnel for his famous quartet (Davis 1989, 233). These personnel experiments from 1959 to 1962, in addition to Coltrane on tenor saxophone, were the following:

Date	Piano	Bass	Drums
Apr. 1959	Cedar Walton	Paul Chambers	Lex Humphries
May 1959	Tommy Flanagan	Paul Chambers	Art Taylor
Nov.-Dec. 1959	Wynton Kelly	Paul Chambers	Jimmy Cobb
Apr.-June 1960	Steve Kuhn	Steve Davis	Pete LaRoca
July 1960	McCoy Tyner	Steve Davis	Pete LaRoca
Sept. 1960	McCoy Tyner	Steve Davis	Billy Higgins
Oct. 1960	McCoy Tyner	Steve Davis	Elvin Jones
July 1961	McCoy Tyner	Reggie Workman	Elvin Jones
Apr. 1962	McCoy Tyner	Jimmy Garrison	Elvin Jones

The group's personnel stabilized in 1962 with Elvin Jones, Tyner, and Jimmy Garrison. Both Tyner and Garrison Philadelphia. During this period, Coltrane began rano saxophone.

It [soprano saxophone] regained its popularity only
after 1960 when John Coltrane began to play it;
virtually every musician was influenced. (Kernfeld
1988, 1:423).

In the 1961 *DownBeat* poll, the Coltrane Quartet with Tyner,
Davis, and Jones won Best New Combo, and Coltrane was
named Best Tenor Saxophonist and Best New Star on Soprano
Saxophone (Davis 1989, 255).

When asked by Frank Kofsky (1970) what to call jazz,
Coltrane's response was this:

> Well, I think it's up to the individual musicians,
> call it what you may, for any reason you may.
> Myself, I recognize the artist. I recognize an
> individual when I see his contribution; and when I
> know a man's sound, well, to me that's him. That's
> this man. That's the way I look at it. Labels, I don't
> bother with. (Coltrane 1964, interview)

Coltrane presents to the listener the impression that there is a
serious mind at work behind the instrument (Levey 1983, 88).

> I don't make a habit of wishing for what I don't
> have, but I often wish I had a lighter nature . . . .
> But you have to be true to your own nature. (Crow
> 1990, 325)

Much of that seriousness and the practice habits that went with it developed in Philadelphia. Coltrane developed around serious musicians such as Jimmy Heath, Benny Golson, and Lee Morgan.

> In the quarter of a century since Trane's [Coltrane's] death, there has not emerged on the jazz scene a great innovator even vaguely his equal. (Nisenson 1993, 224)

I remember seeing Coltrane at the Blue Note in New York. He played the whole set solo. I had never heard anybody do this.

James "Jimmy" Edward Heath

Jimmy Heath—saxophonist, flutist, composer, educator, and arranger—was born in Philadelphia on October 25, 1926, and currently heads the Jazz Studies Department at Queens College, Queens, New York. Heath came from a musical family: his father, Percy Senior, played clarinet in the O. V. Catto marching band; his mother sang in the church choir; his sister, Elizabeth, studied the piano; and his two brothers, Albert and Percy, became outstanding musicians. Heath attended public school in Philadelphia until the sixth grade. When his father lost his job, Heath was sent to live with relatives in Wilmington, North Carolina, where he began his musical training.

> The black high school only offered education for carpentry or brick laying. However, the school's band director was interested in jazz music. In 1939, his father bought him a saxophone [alto]. (Interview, Porter 1995).

Heath studied both in Wilmington, North Carolina, during the winter and Philadelphia, during the summer with local musicians (interview, Porter 1995). A key model for Heath in Philadelphia at that time was Jimmy Oliver. "Benny Golson, John Coltrane, and myself used to listen to him all the time because he was the best saxophonist in the city" (interview, Porter 1995).

Musicians around Philadelphia called Heath "Little Bird" because he analyzed and played so perfectly the bebop repertory created by Charlie "Bird" Parker and Dizzy Gillespie (Taylor 1979, 42). The comparison with Parker and Gillespie ceased when Heath began playing tenor saxophone in 1951 after leaving the Gillespie band. In 1959, after having played in Dizzy Gillespie's big band and sextet from 1949 to 1951, Heath replaced John Coltrane for two months in Miles Davis's quintet. Recordings from this period reveal that Heath's lyrical lines explore the harmonic possibilities of standard chord changes—"The Thumper," recorded September 1959, and *The Riverside Collection*: "Nice People," recorded from 1959 to 1964 (Cook and Morton

1994, 599). According to Lyons and Perlo (1989), Heath's rich, powerful tone and aggressive phrasing resemble the sound of John Coltrane (pp. 263-64).

> Heath's saxophone style owes something to that of Coltrane, but his tone and vibrato are warmer and his melodic lines are usually less ornate (Kernfeld 1988, 1:511).

Heath states the following about Coltrane's practice habits:

> At the time Coltrane was playing with Miles [1955-1959] he worked just about every week and he practiced more than anybody I ever met. So, if he didn't play better than anyone else he would have to be a dumb man. (Interview, Porter 1995).

Heath also states that he did not practice twelve hours a day like Coltrane.

At the age of twenty, Heath had led his own band in Philadelphia, and some of the personnel included Coltrane, Johnny Coles, Nelson Boyd, Willie Dennis, Benny Golson, Specs Wright, and older brother Percy (Giddins, liner notes, 1973).

In an interview with Leonard Feather (1980), Heath talks about his experience in rhythm and blues groups.

> Yes, I have run the gamut of playing music, I've
> played behind r & b people, and Billy Holiday and
> Sarah Vaughan and all the jazz people. Also, I've
> played behind some of the current rock artiste [*sic*]
> who were big stars when I was playing in a house
> band in Philadelphia. It was one of my students
> [Sam Reed] who was leading the band at the
> Uptown Theatre, so I had some experience playing
> behind Sam Cooke, James Brown. (p. 90)

In the late 1940s, Heath began composing and arranging for his own groups and others. Heath was influenced by composers/ arrangers Gil Fuller, Tadd Dameron, and Gil Evans (Giddins, liner notes, 1973).

> More than 50 of his pieces have been recorded
> by some of the premier musicians of our time
> including Milt Jackson, Cannonball Adderley,
> Chet Baker, James Moody, Eddie Harris, Richard
> "Groove" Holmes, Blue Mitchell, and Miles Davis.
> One of Davis' finest albums of the early 1950s
> included young Heath's "CTA," and Miles' version
> of "Gingerbread Boy" found enthusiastic acceptance
> in the sixties. (Ramsey, liner notes, 1979)

Heath wrote about ninety original compositions. Several are jazz standards: "CTA," 1953; "Gemini," 1960; and "Gingerbread

Boy," 1966, which has been his most recorded composition (Feather 1980, 95). Heath is one of the most formidable writers on the American panorama (Williams, liner notes, 1981). Heath has the rare ability to write compositions that are intriguing for the musicians to play and memorable for the listener (Giddins, liner notes, 1973). According to Lyons and Perlo (1989), Heath scores lush chord voicing, counterpoint, and double-time ensemble figures; yet his scores retain the bare rhythmic vitality of hard bop (pp. 263-64). I introduced to the Community College Jazz band some of Heath's arrangements.

Heath states the following about the acceptance of his music.

> I made a whole lot of secret albums. Many of my compositions I did myself, and I thought they were good enough, but without distribution, and without the so-called big name, they never really got around, they're still secrets. (Feather, interview, 1980, 95)

The motivation behind Heath's composing is his strong feelings about the necessity of establishing a repertoire.

There is no jam scene today because there is no common repertoire . . . . We have to establish a common repertoire like the so-called classical people or the traditionalist with their **Saints** [bold Giddins]. (Giddins, liner notes, 1973)

During an interview by Bob Rosenblum (1976), Heath was asked the following questions:

1) How are record dates set up?

    I choose my own musicians or I don't record. I was without a contract for a long period of time. I want control of my music and what I'm gonna play. (p. 3)

2) Can white people play jazz?

    Environment has a lot to do with it . . . . But the general rule is that it comes from an environment of suffering. (p. 3)

Heath's influence extended not only beyond his playing but also to his compositional prowess. He directly influenced Coltrane, Golson, and Morgan, all of whom became leading jazz musicians.

Sidebar: Went to the Northern California Culture Festival held at the Billy Graham Civic Auditorium in San Francisco to hear an original musical, "Rev It Up." It was performed by the youth group of SGI-USA. My sister is a Buddhist.

Benny Golson

Benny Golson—tenor saxophonist, composer, and arranger— was born in Philadelphia on January 26, 1929. Golson grew up in North Philadelphia near Temple University.

> When I was nine I became interested in the piano, and my mother told me I could have lessons as long as I learned to play the organ as well. (Voce, interview, 1982, 8)

At fourteen, Golson heard Arnett Cobb with Lionel Hampton's band play "Flying Home" and began studying tenor saxophone; he also studied the clarinet. Later tenor saxophone influences were Dexter Gordon, Coleman Hawkins, Don Byas (Voce, interview, 1982, 8), and Philadelphian Jimmy Oliver.
According to Voce (interview, 1982),

> in retrospect, the generation that came after Parker and Gillespie was one of the most important in all jazz history, with Getz and Rollins at one end and Clifford Brown and John Coltrane at the other. Right in the middle of it was Benny Golson, one of the most imaginative and elegant of all jazz composers. (p. 8)

After graduating from Benjamin Franklin High School in 1947, Golson entered Howard University in Washington, DC, to study music education. At Howard University, Golson started to write for the University's jazz band, which made it possible for him to hear his compositions. "That was fantastic" (Golson, Voce, interview, 1982).

Golson states the following about his early attempts at writing music:

> I wanted to play the solos from the records so bad and I wanted to remember the notes but wasn't always sure, so I devised a way of putting them down on paper. Each note the soloist played I wrote a little goose egg, just a little circle, no time to it or anything. Only I knew what the time was. Eventually, I thought that, although it worked all right for me, it was no good because nobody else could play it. So I learned how to put the note values down, and once I could do that I thought it would be nice if other people could play as a group from what I wrote down. (Voce, interview, 1982)

Golson's first composition was called "The Maharajah and the Blues," which was in the style of Dizzy's "Night in Tunisia" (Voce, interview, 1982). Percy Heath's comment was "It doesn't sound right." Golson stated that he wrote a lot of bad ones in those early years. In 1951, while in Bull Moose Jackson's band,

Golson met composer/arranger Tadd Dameron, whose work was an influence on Golson's compositional style (Kernfeld, 1988, vol. 1, p. 436).

> After three years at college training to be a teacher I decided that wasn't for me. I entered college in September 1947 and came out in the early fifties. I had decided to jump in at the deep end and become a professional musician. (Voce, interview, 1982)

Golson played with the following groups after college: Lionel Hampton, 1953; Earl Bostic, 1954-1956; Dizzy Gillespie, 1956-1957; and the Jazz Messengers, 1958-59 (Kernfeld, 1988, 1:436). When Golson replaced Ernie Wilkins in Gillespie's band, Gillespie asked Golson to write charts for the band. "He [Gillespie] had a tremendous effect on me, even though he played trumpet and I played saxophone" (Voce, interview, 1982a, 6).

Golson replaced Jackie McLean in the Jazz Messengers in February 1958 because McLean had difficulty getting a "police card," which he needed in order to work in the New York night clubs (Voce, interview, 1982a, 6). Because Blakey's management skills were poor, Blakey asked Golson to become band manager. Golson replaced the band personnel with three Philadelphians: Lee Morgan, trumpet; Bobby Timmons, piano; and Jymie "James" Merritt, double bass. Golson was replaced by Wayne Shorter in 1959 (Voce, interview, 1982a, 6). From 1959 to 62, with Art Farmer, Golson was leader of the Jazztet, a group that proved a successful vehicle for Golson's new compositions. These bands were some of the finest of the fifties.

Quincy Jones helped Golson secure positions in film and television, composing music for Universal, Columbia, Paramount, and 20th Century Fox for about nine years (Voce, interview, 1982a, 7; Kernfeld 1988, 1:437).

> Although I still write jazz compositions, I suppose the
> most immediate success I had with my writing was
> at the time I was with Art Blakey (Voce 1982a, 7).

While with the Jazz Messengers, Golson composed some of his finest compositions: "Whisper Not," "Along Came Betty," "Blues March," and "Are You Real." However, Golson wrote his most played composition, "I Remember Clifford," while he was with the Gillespie Band. Gillespie recorded "I Remember Clifford" with his band in July 1957 at Newport, Verve 513754-2CD (Cook and Morton 1994, 496), but Lee Morgan had recorded it first—March 24, 1957, in the "Lee Morgan Volume III," Blue Note 1557. Golson states the following about "I Remember Clifford":

> I thought it would be a good tribute if I could
> write a song that was in a similar style to the way
> that he played, and I thought, boy, that would be a
> challenge. (Voce, interview, 1982a, 6)

Yes I do work a long time at my composition usually. But in contrast to all the honing and polishing I did on something like "I Remember Clifford," "Whisper Not" came to me in about 20 minutes! (Voce, interview, 1982a, 6)

Golson states the following about composing:

Each note has to mean something to me now, but when I was younger I just turned them out one after another. (Voce, interview, 1982a, 6).

I've always loved Brahms and Chopin for their intense melodic qualities. (Voce, interview, 1982a, 6)

Three of Golson's compositions—"Stablemates," "Whisper Not," and "I Remember Clifford"—have become canons in African American classical music. When he joined Art Blakey's Jazz Messengers in 1958, he brought his number 2 pencil as well as his tenor saxophone.

Lee Morgan

Lee Morgan—trumpeter and composer—(b. in Philadelphia, July 10, 1938; d. in New York, February 19, 1972) studied privately at Mastbaum Technical High School. He began working professionally at fifteen, leading his own group (*DownBeat*, editorial, March 30, 1972). Morgan participated in the many jam sessions that were popular in Philadelphia, and his skills were admired by prominent visiting musicians.

During the summer of 1956, at the age of eighteen, Morgan joined Dizzy Gillespie's big band and remained until early 1958. Later that year, he was asked by Benny Golson, along with Bobby Timmons and Jymie Merritt, to join Art Blakey's Jazz Messengers. This group recorded some of Morgan's finest work. Morgan left in 1961 and spent a year in Philadelphia, working with Jimmy Heath and others (*DownBeat*, editorial, March 30, 1972).

> Hailed as the heir to Clifford Brown when he first became nationally known, Morgan was initially influenced by Dizzy Gillespie, Fats Navarro and Brown. (*DownBeat*, editorial, March 30, 1972)

Morgan was a supremely confident player, sometimes given to flashy display, but his work matured with the years, gaining emotional depth without losing its characteristic exuberance (*DownBeat*, editorial, March 30, 1972).

Morgan's biggest success was a blues composition, "Sidewinder," which became a hit record in 1963. However, Morgan did not succumb to the temptation to commercialize his music; he remained a dedicated jazz player. Like many

Philadelphia African American jazz musicians, Morgan was serious about African American classical music.

In addition to many albums under his own name, Morgan recorded prolifically as a featured sideman with many famous musicians, including three sessions with John Coltrane.

1) April 4, 1957 (Blue Note, BLP1559 Johnny Griffin/A Blowing Session) (Morgan and Coltrane were sidemen.)
2) September 15, 1957 (Blue Note, BLP1577 John Coltrane/ Blue Train)
3) September 9, 1958 (Audio tape of a jam session held at the Plaza Hotel in New York City) (Included Billy Strayhorn on piano) (Fujioka 1995)

Of the three sessions, John Coltrane/Blue Train became most notable. This session included Philly Joe Jones on drums (Fujioka 1995, 76).

After an interview with Lee Morgan (1972), Mike Bourne stated the following about Morgan:

> Interviewing Lee Morgan proved easy—not simply because he was loquacious, but because he knew his mind so well he would speak it without any hesitation, and do so with great insight and passion. (p. 11)

On the subject of jazz in America, Morgan states the following:

> This dilemma was two-fold, or rather two-faced: lack of respect, and a lack of proportion between black American art and the general American culture. (Bourne 1972, 11)

Morgan goes on to state that

> if it wasn't for music, this country would have blown up a long time ago; in fact, the whole world. (Bourne 1972, 11)

These four Philadelphia African American musicians produced some of the finest African American classical music ever, and Philadelphia contributed heavily to the education, socialization, and venues for their five stages of development. Lee Morgan was a fine classical musician in high school. He played in the All-City band and in 1954 was a member of the Pennsylvania All-State Concert Band, which was held in Wallingford, Pennsylvania. He and I made State Band that year. In fact, I drove him to a gig he had after the concert in Norristown, Pennsylvania. Lee Morgan was doing in 1954 what Wynton Marsalis is doing today, playing both classical and jazz music. It's unfortunate we lost him so early. I was speaking with him at the Aqua Lounge on Fifty-Second street about two months before he was killed by his new friend, and he talked about how she was acting as his business agent, and he said, "She was taking care of business."

Dealing with music, it is important to have a supportive family, especially a wife or significant other. Look at Sonny Rollins, Dizzy Gillespie, Louis Armstrong, and Jimmy Heath; they all had strong support from their wives. Art Bakley's wife would set up his drum kit before every performance. It helps to have the support of one's family because musicians live haphazard lives, being on the road so often.

CHAPTER FIVE

Having played in the All-City Junior High Orchestra for three years, the next step was the All-City Senior High Band and Orchestra. The band was conducted by Dr. Edwin E. Heilakka. The orchestra was conducted by Dr. Louis G. Werson, who was also the director of music education. The assistant directors for the division were F. Edna Davis and George P. Spangler. These groups, including the All-City choir, rehearsed every Tuesday night from 7:00-9:00 p.m. The band and orchestra rehearsed at Northeast High School, located at Eighth and Lehigh Avenue in North Philadelphia. The choir, which my wife, Eloise, was a member, rehearsed at Dobbins Vocational High School, was conducted by F. Edna Davis, and was located at Twenty-Second and Lehigh Avenue.

These groups were elite. They were made up of the very best music students in Philadelphia. Many of them went on to Curtis Institute of Music, Julliard School of Music, Eastman School of Music, Temple's School of Music, and West Chester's School of Music. Some went on to become professional musicians right after high school like trumpeters Lee Morgan, Ted Curson, and the Grimes brothers, Henry and Leon. The competition for membership and chairs was very competitive. First chair was the goal, and for African Americans, this was a challenge socially and musically.

There was also competition between schools. During this time, the main competition was between Southern, located at Broad and Snyder; West Philadelphia, located at Forty-Seventh and Walnut; Mastbaum Technical, located at Frankford and Clementine; and Central High School, located at Ogontz and Olney Avenue. There was also girls high, located at the time at 1700 and Spring Garden Streets, and Overbrook, located at Fifty-Ninth and Lancaster Avenue. My main competition came from the Italians from South Philadelphia High School, particularly a clarinetist whose name was Genovese. He came from a family of musicians who went on to play in major symphony orchestras in the United States. One night, he would play first chair; the next week, I would be in the chair. We played musical chairs. Students from Southern would brag about their repertoire. They claimed they played the "Rite of Spring" by Stravinsky. This might have been true because many of them went on to become professional classical players. Some are now playing in the Philadelphia Orchestra. African Americans who went on to play in symphony orchestras were Ann Hobson, harp, Boston Symphony; Robert Joel, oboe, Denver Symphony; Booker Rowe, violin, and Reynard Edwards, viola Philadelphia Orchestra. Reynard graduated from Overbrook.

Tuesdays were the most important days besides Saturday morning lessons with Mr. Liberio. It would take about an hour to get to Northeast High School from West Philadelphia. The ride was interesting because I met many of the African American students who were interested in music. We would talk about music and girls. The Philadelphia Transportation Company (PTC) was the public transportation company at the time. It later became the Southeastern Public Transportation Agency (SEPTA). We would take the Frankford train, transfer to the Broad Street train, then transfer to the Lehigh trolley to Eighth and Lehigh. The choir took the trolley west to Twenty-Second Street. Even though my time was divided between music and basketball, I did manage to find time for a few dates.

Every year there were two major concerts for the All-City groups, "Schools on Parade" and a concert at the Academy of Music located at Broad and Locust Streets, home of the Philadelphia Orchestra. "Schools on Parade" included the All-City groups plus selected school groups. It was cosponsored by the school district and *The Philadelphia Bulletin*. This was a big production held at the Philadelphia Civic Center. The academy concert was only for All-City groups. Of course, it was a formal concert. This was a great honor to perform on the same stage as the Philadelphia Orchestra and to go backstage to see the traveling cases used by the musicians, the dressing rooms for guest artists, and the conductor Eugene Ormandy.

Some of the compositions the All-City orchestra performed at these concerts were the following: The Carnival of the Animals by Camille Saint-Saens, Night on Bald Mountain by Modest Petrovich Mussorgsky, Romanian Rhapsody no. 1 by Georges Ernesto, Symphonie Espagnole by Edouard Lalo, and Concerto in

A Minor by Robert Schumann. Louis Lanza was the violin soloist in Lalo, and I did the clarinet solo at the end of the Mussorgsky. I can't recall the soloist in the Schumann.

Sidebar: Last night, I was at Orlieb's Jazz House and was talking with Sam Reed. He remembered music he had played in All-City. Sam was the former band leader at the Uptown Theater at Board and Susquehanna Avenue (September 1, 2001).

One of my best friends I met in All-City was Aldo Bettelli. He played the clarinet and the saxophone. He went to Bartram High School. I met him when I was in the tenth grade and he was in the twelfth grade. We also studied with the same clarinet teacher, Mr. Liberio. He was my musical mentor. Aldo was playing first chair when I got into the orchestra. His technique was flawless. He also had a beautiful sound. We spent many hours playing duets and talking about life over spaghetti his mother would fix at his house in the 6200 block of Lansdowne Avenue.

Aldo attended Temple University on a board of education scholarship, the Curtis Institute of Music, studying with Anthony Gigliotti. He went on to play with the US Army Band "Pershing Own" in Washington, DC. My son George Jr. was a member of this band for twenty years. After returning to Philadelphia, Aldo auditioned for the second clarinet chair for the Philadelphia Orchestra. Aldo came in second. The nights before the Curtis and orchestra auditions, he wanted me to critique him and help him pick out a reed. For the Curtis audition, we spent time fine-tuning the slow movements of Mozart's Clarinet Quintet and Concerto. For the orchestra audition, we concentrated on the passages from Maurice Ravel's Daphnis et Chloe Ballet Suite no. 2 and the solo from Nicolas Rimsky-Korsakoff's Le Coq D'Or Suite.

These are some of the more difficult clarinet passages in the orchestra canon. He wanted me to listen because he knew I was familiar with the orchestral repertoire. He knew I would be honest. I had played some of the repertoire at West Chester as first clarinetist; besides, we had played so much together. Aldo died in a matter of years after the orchestra audition. I believed not making the orchestra shortened his life. I think I would have been very disappointed also if I didn't teach music; I have always thought of myself as a teacher first and a player second. When I perform, I think of myself as a teacher playing the instrument. Performing does not hold the same curiosity that teaching has. I really started teaching in elementary school, helping students when they had a problem with the instrument or the music. I have been doing this ever since. I was not asked. Aldo's life was playing the clarinet and being a member of the orchestra, like my life is about music education. I lost a wonderful friend and mentor.

When I was in high school, there were opportunities for me to perform with other groups like the Philadelphia Concert Orchestra, Philadelphia Youth Orchestra, Elks and Post bands, Mummers day parades, teas, recitals, competitions, and district and state bands.

Sidebar: Visited with Dr. Dewey Royal, a former trombonist with the North Philadelphia Youth Symphony Orchestra in the '70s, which was conducted by Robert Joell. After attending Mastbaum Technical High School, he went to Cheyney University, then Brandeis University where he received a master's in biology. After being diagnosed with multiple sclerosis, he earned a PhD in biology from the University of Iowa. He is a researcher at the Nelson Biological Laboratories at the State University—Rutgers in New Brunswick, New Jersey (August 10, 2001).

Pennsylvania Music Educators Association (PMEA) sponsored district and state festivals. Pennsylvania is divided up into twelve districts and six regions. Each district and region held festivals that culminated in the All-State Festival. You could make All-State by ranking high at district and region auditions. I made All-State band in my junior and senior year. Students from Philadelphia didn't participate in PMEA festivals because the Division of Music felt All-City was a better or equal experience for Philadelphia students. Philadelphia also did not participate in the Pennsylvania Athletic Conference. We had the public and Catholic conferences. Mr. Loper, my band director, supported PMEA. This experience broadened my perspective of the bigger picture in terms of competition in music. I learned there were some very fine players throughout the state. It kept me from becoming provincial in my thinking about music.

In my junior year, I got very ill with some kind of virus just before I was to go to All-State band. The night before I was to leave for the festival in Sayre, Pennsylvania, my father had the doctor come to the house. The doctor recommended that I stay home. My father sensed my disappointment and told the doctor, "If he is going to die, let him die playing music." I took the Greyhound Bus to Sayre, Pennsylvania. It was a wonderful festival for me because I made solo chair. I was the only African American in the band. The festivals lasted three days, and band members were housed in private homes, not in hotels. I stayed with a Caucasian family. During the three days, I do not remember seeing any African Americans. In my senior year, there was a scheduling conflict with the Philadelphia Youth Symphony and All-State band concert. So that year, I played the All-City concert at the Academy of Music in the afternoon and the All-State concert in the evening at Wallingford, Pennsylvania.

The board of education gave music scholarships to graduating seniors. I did not receive one. Two students from Overbrook received two of the ten scholarships. One became a music therapist; the other became a medical doctor. I guess they had better grades than I, but I was the better musician. My father thought it was a racial issue. I really did not think along those lines because I had so many white friends that I had met while playing music. One African American received a music scholarship that year. His name is Clarence Watson from West Philadelphia High School. He went on to Temple University and earned a degree in music education. He became master trombonist and fine music educator in New Jersey.

I give much credit to Mr. Chance and Mr. Loper for helping me become a music educator and a better person. One of the things I remember about the music curriculum at Overbrook was the theory courses. It was taught by Mr. Kasse. He taught harmony using a numbers system. We would partly write by using numbers. For example, I—IV—V—I progression would be harmonized by using 8-8-7-8, 5-6-5-5, and 3-4-2-3 with 1-4-5-1 in the bass. I can't recall if I did any singing in theory class. When I went to college, I was behind because I had very little experience in sightsinging.

My two primary interests in high school were music first and basketball second. I played for the Clover Coasters in two leagues. The team was made up of guys from West Philadelphia who lived in walking distance from Haddington Recreation Center, located at Forty-Seventh and Haverford Avenue across the street from Brooks School. One of the smartest players on the team was Nathaniel Winslow, "Peanut," who lived down the "bottom" on the 5100 block of Summer Street. He was our coach on the court. He never played in high school, but he had a complete knowledge of the game. We won a lot of games because we played smart basketball. We called the coach Doc. His last name was Randolph. Doc worked for the city as a crime-prevention officer. We didn't know where he lived. As near we got to knowing where he lived was somewhere in the "bottom." In fact, many of the team members did not know what Doc did until we were older. Doc had a good knowledge of the game and people. One time after practice, Doc asked me, "How many hands do you have?"

I said, "Two." He said, "Why don't you use them?" He was an unlicensed psychologist. He taught me the fundamentals and the importance of using both hands. He told me to start doing things with my left hand, like carrying my instrument and school books and opening doors. I became ambidextrous, using both hands on defense and offence. It helped me to become an excellent defensive player. I had to because my offensive game was average. I got the junk points: layups. I had a reputation as a defensive player and a rebounder. I was six four and weighed about 184 pounds. I had to play smart because most of the guys were bigger and better than I was. Basketball taught me one of life's great lessons: how to win and lose while always doing your best.

The best African American high school and college players came to Haddington every Saturday morning to play half-court games of five on a team. For the first game, two of the best players would pick their team. The loser would have to sit and wait to be chosen for another team. If the score was tied at twenty, the winning team had to win by four points, just like they do in tennis with match points. Someone had to call "winners" to pick the next five players. Some of these games became legendary in city basketball especially when players came from North and South Philadelphia for bragging rights.

Some Saturday mornings, there would be some of the finest players on the court like Wilt Chamberlain, Walt Hazzard, Guy Rogers, Claud Gross, Ti Parham, Wayne Hightower, John Tatum, John Chaney, "Tricks" Murray, Wally Jones, Howard Lear, Earl "the Pearl" Monroe, and Jackie Moore. There were other outstanding players from Overbrook, like the Sadler brothers, Ira Davis, Howard "Bitty" Johnson, Marty Hughes, Vincent Miller, and Thomas Fitzhugh. The players from West Philadelphia High School were Reese Murray, Bob Hall, Cortez Manning, and the Showell brothers. It was an honor to be picked to play with them.

I would come after things got started because I took my clarinet lesson on Saturday mornings. I would get to Haddington about eleven thirty. It was fine because the guys knew I was studying music. Saturdays were both exciting and magical: music in the morning, basketball and the Metropolitian Opera in the afternoon, and the Philadelphia Orchestra and jazz at night. Tuesdays with All-City and Saturdays were utopia. Some of these players went on to play in the NBA, and when I see any of them now, I always thank them for helping me become the person I am today. I see many of them during the summer at the Sonny Hill basketball league. If anyone wants to know anything about basketball, come to Temple's McGonical Hall and ask Sonny Hill or anyone at the game.

CHAPTER SIX

I started West Chester State Teachers College on September 1954. Temple rejected me. I was not asked. I never did find out why, but it might have been my grades, not my music preparation. By this time, I had completed the complete Kolse, Rose, Rode, and Bettoney-Baermann methods and was beginning the Calvaline method. Also, I had prepared the Mozart, two Weber concerti, and the "Rigoletto Fantasy" by Bassi. I was still studying with Mr. Liberio. I applied at West Chester because I had heard they had a music education curriculum. When I went for the interview and audition at the registrar, Dr. B. Paul Ross asked me why I didn't apply at Cheyney State Teachers College, an African American college near West Chester. I told him that Cheyney did not have a music education curriculum and I wanted to be a music educator. My goal was to teach music in Philadelphia. Later that day, I auditioned for Mr. Paul Carson, the marching and concert band director. I passed and was enrolled in the music education curriculum. I think he might have remembered me from All-State Band.

The dorm was the "Eisenhower Barracks," which consisted of two floors with about ten rooms on each floor. Heating was supplied by a coal stove, which sometimes didn't function very well. During my freshman year, hunger was the first priority, not heat. I would go home on the weekends to get a care package from my mother plus five dollars of spending money, which included the carfare to get back to West Chester. We would eat the care package that Sunday night. I learned to eat melted cheese-on-toast. The students called it something else. It was a staple at the college. At meals, we sat in banquet style of ten with a waiter who were mainly athletes. After the food was passed around, I always tried to get seconds. Because I was doing marching band, orchestra, and basketball along with my music classes, I was burning up a lot of energy. Mrs. Joyce became one of my best friends. She was the dining room supervisor. In my senior year, she would let me into the dining room for free because at the time, I was a commuting student, doing student teaching and evening rehearsals. Between the "Eisenhower Barracks" and being hungry most of the time, I survived my freshman year, but I was put on academic probation at the end of the semester.

That summer, my father asked me if I wanted a summer job. I said yes. I had summer jobs before, working in small stores and shops of my father's friends, but nothing had prepared me for this summer job. He got me a job working for Keystone Concrete as a laborer. My first job was on Lawrence Road off West Chester Pike. My assignment was to dig an eight-foot-square hole eight feet deep. I thought this would be easy, no problem. I started around 7:30 a.m., and by 2:00 p.m., I was throwing dirt over my head, and I stand at six four. While I was doing this, I saw my father standing at the top of the hole, and he asked me how I was doing. Out of pride, I said, "Fine." But inside, I said to myself that if all I have to do was read some books to become a music educator when I went back to West Chester Teachers College, that is what I would do. This changed my whole concept about what I had to do to educate myself. I didn't become an honor roll student, but I did much better.

Fourteen African Americans were admitted to West Chester Teachers College in 1954, and all fourteen graduated in 1958. We helped each other. For example, I helped Alice Tucker, who was from Ardmore, with her music, and she helped me with my writing. I benefited from these fourteen African Americans. They were so important to me graduating that I would like to acknowledge them. They were F. Louise Blackwell from Penllyn; Viola H. Bradford from Coatesville; my fraternity brother, basketball teammate, and roommate, Carson Carr from Philadelphia; Fannie M. Coles, Epsie M. Holmes, Florence J. Jenkins, Eleanor L. Lewis, William C. Polk, Barbara G. Potts— all also from Philadelphia; Thomas M. Cooper from Republic, Pennsylvania; E. Dolores James from Penllyn; Vivian Carter Thomas from West Chester; and my proofreader, Alice Tucker.

The following was taken from the *West Chester Alumni Newsletter* dated June 2002.

Hollywood talent manager, Dolores Robinson '58 [E. Dolores James] shared some sage career advice with the Class of 2002 when she took the podium as this year's commencement speaker. Her career path began in Philadelphia with teaching, then motherhood, then public relations and broadcasting on KYW. She left for L.A. in 1974, saw an opportunity to launch several actors' careers and opened her own management company in 1976 called Dolores Robinson Entertainment. Her first client was Levon Burton, and she quickly built her roster to include Wesley Snipes, Martin Sheen, Rosie Perez, Pierce Brosnam, Linda Fiorentino, Kadeem Hardison, Jason Patrici. She also handles the career of her daughter Holly Robinson Peete.

Richard Lawrence was from West Philadelphia, and I interviewed him about his time at West Chester. He was a year behind me.

Interview with Richard Lawrence from Phila. December 18, 2001.

Richard Lawrence attended West Philadelphia High as did Carson Carr. I asked Richard if his high school prepared him academically for college. His answer was "I could have been prepared in high school, but I chose not to prepare myself in that I was the type of student who was interested in getting by and doing the social kinds of things in high school as opposed to the academics." He went on to say he felt if he had addressed the academics, he would have been in the top tier of his class. West Philadelphia High School's Jewish population was about the same as Overbrook, 65 percent.

When Richard came to West Chester in 1957, the college admitted approximately thirty African Americans. I mentioned to Richard that my class only had fourteen African Americans. His response was that historically, West Chester had been admitting twenty-five to thirty-five African Americans. He felt that it was difficult to determine the number of African American students because most were commuters. There were very few places for African Americans to live in West Chester. The only student I knew who lived in West Chester was Rose Devone, and her mother worked for the college.

I asked Richard about the social conditions.

> Poor. There was a good camaraderie among all of the minority students, or let me say most of the minority students. However, things in general were not very good because there was very little that you could do off campus. You could go to the movies but there were other places in the town that you couldn't actually go to like the restaurants in the town. When you went out at night you couldn't go to the establishments that they [whites] could go to. I often remember as a youngster going to West Chester with my father and we would go in the restaurants that he was servicing and there would be no people of color in those establishments. (Interview, December 2001)

His father was an exterminator.

Richard went on to say he could not understand how I, as a music student, could play basketball on the college level. Richard started out as a health and physical education major but graduated as an elementary education major because it was found that he was diabetic.

Richard also had a bad relationship with the dean of men, Dean Killinger. He wanted Richard out of school because he had parked his car in a restricted area on campus so he could get to the dining hall before it closed. He received a ticket. When he went to see the dean about the ticket, the secretary said, "You're in for it." When he finally met with Dean Killinger, he told Richard, "Pack up your clothes. You are being thrown out of school immediately." He was not allowed to speak or defend himself. He went to the track coach and told him what happened. The coach went to the president of the college to get Richard reinstated. The dean did not speak to Richard during the remaining time he was a student at the college. I was told by the same dean to cut my hair because he said I looked like Jesus. Afros were in style for African Americans at the time.

Richard remembered first seeing me winning a talent contest at Greater St. Matthew United Methodist Church when I was about fifteen. He remembered me playing basketball at Haddington and the Dunlap school yard. He also remembered doing my daughters Ina's and Gloria's diapers when we were living at Fifty-Sixth and Race in a third-floor apartment. He was pledged to my fraternity, Alpha Phi Alpha. After several teaching and administrative positions in the Philadelphia School District, he took a disability retirement due to blindness. Richard retired as a special education supervisor.

Because there weren't many social activities for African American students on campus, on weekends, most of us went home when we could. When we stayed on campus, we would socialize at Rose Devon's house in West Chester. One reason why I liked these Saturday evening socials was because they would let me pantomime jazz artists like vibraphonists Lionel Hampton and Milt Jackson. My favorite pantomimes were Hampton's recording of "Star Dust" recorded at the Hollywood Bowl in 1947: "Gene Norman presents JUST JAZZ Concert, Lionel Hampton All Stars and the All Stars." The All Stars included Willie Smith, alto saxophone; Charlie Shavers, trumpet; Slam Stewart, bass; Barney Kessel, guitar; Tommy Todd, piano; Lee Young, drums; and Corky Corcoran, tenor saxophone (Decca DL 7013). This is my favorite improvised jazz solo. The other pantomime was the vibraphone solos by Milt Jackson with the Modern Jazz Quartet with John Lewis, pianist and composer; Connie Kay, drums; and Percy Heath, bass.

We also went to the one movie theater in West Chester. It was segregated. One evening, Carson and I decided to integrate the movie. We took the risk because he and I had pictures and stories written up in the West Chester newspaper, Carson for being on the basketball team and I about involvement in musical activities and basketball on campus. We decided that if anyone asked about us sitting downstairs in the white section, we would say we were on the basketball team. No one asked, so we integrated the movie theater in West Chester. We didn't think it was a big deal; in fact, we didn't tell anybody what we had done. I was not asked.

Dr. Madeline Cartwright, an outstanding administrator in the Philadelphia School District, was in the same class as Richard Lawrence at West Chester. She has written a book, *For the Children: Lessons from a Visionary Principal*, about her experiences in the district.

Interview with Dr. Madeline Cartwright, January 4, 2002

When I asked Dr. Cartwright, a commuting student when I went to West Chester, if her high school education at S. Horace Scott in Coatsville, Pennsylvania, prepared her for college, she stated, "Yes, it did." She went on to say that she was given tests they were expected that they would have in college. The school was 90 percent white, and only 10 percent of the remaining African Americans were in the academic track. She remembers about twenty-five African Americans in her class at West Chester. I asked her about the social conditions at the college. She states the following:

> Well George, to be perfectly honest, I didn't do a lot of socializing. I came to school and left and went home. I worked the entire time that I was going to school. (Interview, January 2004)

Like me, Dr. Cartwright started teaching early.

I probably was a teacher all my life. Even though I was the youngest in the family, I had a little school in my basement when I was a little kid and other children came to the school and their parents sent them because I taught. I guess I was about maybe . . . 12 years old. (Interview, January 2002)

I remember visiting Madeline during the West Chester years at her home in Coatsville, Pennsylvania. I was driving one night west on Route 30 and almost crashed the car because I thought I was going to be hit by a train going east that ran parallel to the highway. I did not know there was a curve in the highway. In my senior year, Madeline and a group from Philadelphia commuted in my father's two-door Ford car.

Dr. Cartwright did for elementary education what I did for music education, motivating students to achieve beyond expected norms. I asked Dr. Cartwright what she remembered most about her experience at West Chester State Teachers College.

I think the thing that sticks out in my mind most of all is that the staff seemed to be surprised that I could be the student that I was and yet come from a public school.

So often instructors, and more than once, instructors said to me or say to the class, "Now you can look at Ms. Berger [Dr. Cartwright] and see

that she was not a product of the public schools."
(Interview, January 2002)

She continued, "I think that sometimes they gave me the feeling that they felt that African American students were not expected to be up to their standards intellectually." Dr. Cartwright felt, when she graduated, she was prepared to be a top-notch educator.

At the present time, I'm mentoring her grandson, Jared Cartwright. He is studying piano, clarinet, and chamber music at the Settlement Music School. During the interview, she stated "I've watched you as you mentored Jared, how his enthusiasm and appreciation for music grew as a result of his relationship with you." At the end of the interview, I related Dr. Cartwright's visit to my music methods class at Cheyney University. One of my students seemed to be disinterested in her presentation about "Developing a Plan for One's Education." Dr. Cartwright said to the student, "How can you sleep as good as I am? Do you know I make . . . per hour for what I'm doing." After retiring from the Philadelphia School District, Dr. Cartwright became an educational motivational speaker.

I had some wonderful professors, but most of the students seem to be better prepared for college, like my friend Robert Ambs. One of the best academic teachers I had was Professor Clark. She was my English professor for two years. She taught English composition and literature. She was a model teacher: she was never absent, used perfect diction, and had prefect appearance; she had complete control of the class and herself. She would pass out materials, and there would be no extras. She was that precise. She passed me with four Ds. I will never forget this great teacher of English. I wish I would have written those spelling words a hundred times and learned English grammar at Brooks School. I would have great ideas, but spelling would stop me from putting them down on paper. Writing has always been a challenge for me, but interestingly, reading has always been a pleasure. I read two or three books a month. I think Professor Clark would be proud of me today.

My first music class was solfeggio sightsinging, which met three times a week. Seats were assigned alphabetically, and I was assigned to the first seat. Robert Ambs was in the second seat. He was Caucasian. Robert was from Philadelphia and went to a Roman Catholic high school at Board and Vine Streets. Robert was a fine flutist. We sat next to each other for four years. We became the best of friends because he had the academics and I had the music. He was a fine human being. When you saw me, you saw Robert. Robert and I played flute duets, which I would transpose on the clarinet. This helped me with C transposition and playing in the altissimo register of my instrument.

Robert had an amazing memory. He would buy textbooks at the beginning of the semester, and at the end of the semester, they still looked like brand-new textbooks. I think he sold some of them back as new books. Robert kept his music books. I had to keep most of my books. Robert would often ask me over the four years, "How come you don't know this?" I interviewed Robert at his home back in January 2002.

Robert Ambs was well prepared for academic challenges at West Chester. He graduated from a Roman Catholic high school. He studied flute with John Krell, who played in the Philadelphia Orchestra. Robert didn't have the benefit of All-City band or orchestra that I had, and he didn't participate in PMEA. After talking about the ten-cent drafts, we drank while studying for midterms and finals. Robert shared some stories about me during our years at West Chester.

> Well, I remember that you got me interested in studying with Mr. Anthony Liberio . . . because I wanted to get better on the clarinet and I heard you performing and was impressed . . . and the fact you used that crystal mouthpiece, and used to really enjoy getting together for duets. (Interview, January 2002)

Robert continues,

> We did our share of horsing around and everything, but we really got down to business at rehearsals like especially orchestra and concert band, and woodwind quintet. Just like maybe, just for fun a minute or so, like playing a tone higher or a tone lower, and seeing if the conductor

would catch it, which, of course, he usually did.
(Interview, January 2002)

I think we all tried that at one time or another in our development as musicians. Robert also remembers being a little shaken up when I got knocked unconscious playing basketball. We both had the same voice teacher, Mr. Sweet, and piano teacher, Ms. Gottlieb. She was a great teacher for me because she would let me sight-read a lot of music, and because of this, I did a lot of accompanying for general and senior recitals. Before midterm and final exams, she would assign me a piece to learn for juries. We both didn't take private lessons at the college. What I remember about Robert is how he knew all these routes to get to school. This was important because many times we would be running late while going to a performance at the college.

In solfege class, Ms. Ashenfelter, the professor, asked me to sing a pitch she had played on the piano, which I could not do. I didn't have a clue, and neither did Robert. I knew at this point, we were in this together. We have known each other since West Chester. Today, he has retired from music education as an instrumental teacher and now does instrumental repair. To this day, he repairs my clarinets.

After I learned how to match pitches, the next problem was the Italian solfege syllables. I think this was the first time I had run into a musical situation that I really had to do some serious work. After working very diligently on the solfege exercises, one day in class, I noticed that one of the exercises looked familiar. It was the principal theme from the fourth movement of Brahms's Symphony no. 1 in C Minor. I had played this movement in All-City Orchestra. I put the two together, and solfege has become one of my best musical tools. I hope that no instrumental music student would not have to go through what I did to learn how to use solfege and not have the experience of singing. I was not asked.

College choir was a wonderful experience because I was able to find my voice classification. I am a baritone. As an instrumentalist, it was exciting singing the melismatic passages, particularly contrapuntal music from the baroque period. One composition we sang was Johann Sebastian Bach's "Christmas Oratorio." Christmas season at West Chester was dominated by choral music and the White Supper. Dr. Jones was the concert choir director. Before Christmas vacation, there would be a candlelit supper. The women dressed in white gowns, and the men wore tuxes or dark suits. This was followed by the "Choral Service" performed by all the choral groups in the music department in Swope Hall Auditorium. The highlight of the Carol Service was the solo singing of "O Holy Night" by an honor voice student.

Christmas season was also the time for partying and drinking. On the day of the White Supper and Carol Service, money was collected to buy liquor, and the amount collected dictated what kind of liquor was bought. Some years, it was just wine or beer. One year, I was chosen to help carry the liquor back to "Eisenhower Barracks." Somehow I dropped one of the bottles, and it broke. Thank goodness that I didn't have all the bottles. The brothers were kind to me. I was not asked *again*.

The marching band practiced five days a week, and it was an all-male marching band of sixty members. The directors were Mr. Paul Carson and Dr. Antonowich. Mr. Carson was the calmest director I have ever worked under. He very seldom raised his voice above a normal speaking voice. Mr. Carson would use psychology to get our attention by saying something like "I heard that Millersville State Teachers College's band director told the band that they had a better half-time show than West Chester." Then he would ask the question, "Is that true?" The band would respond no. Those kinds of statements would motivate the band even when we knew the statement was not true.

Sidebar: It will be unreal to drive to New York and not see the Twin Towers as a road marker (September 11, 2001).

According to the 1954 yearbook, West Chester's marching band was "the best small band in the country." The band was a fast high-stepping organization similar to the Florida State A & M band. The band not only looked good, but we also sounded like a concert band on the field. We also performed in parades in the surrounding communities, and in 1954, the band performed a half-time show for the Philadelphia Eagles at Shibe Park, located at Twenty-Second and Lehigh Avenue. I believe my parents attended the game. Because I was Philadelphia fan, it was exciting to be playing at an Eagles game. I was so impressed by the size of the players and the stark size of the injuries that I almost forgot to get into position to start the half-time show. I played my "Boosey and Hawkes" clarinet during marching band season. Marching was not one of my favorite music activities at West Chester. I was an orchestral player. I would select a reed at the beginning of marching band season, and I would use the same reed for the entire marching band season. The reed didn't sound so good by the last game. Participating in marching bands for seven years, including three years at Overbrook, I made a commitment never to march again. It was not my thing. I was only asked once by Mr. Liberio to march in an Italian Festival parade, which I did out of respect for him. When I see *The Godfather* movie, I am reminded of that parade.

The college symphony orchestra was different because of two things: one, the music, and two, the conductor. Mr. Powell Middleton was a fine musician. His primary instruments were the string bass and french horn. The orchestra met on Wednesday evenings from seven to nine, and it was the apex of the week for me. Some of the repertoire the orchestra performed were Le Coq D'or Suite by Rimsky-Korsakoff, Piano Concerto no. 2 by Serge Rachmaninoff, Die Meistersinger von Nurnburg by Richard Wagner, Symphony no. 4 in G by Antonin Dvorak, and Piano Concerto no. 4 in G by Ludwig Van Beethoven. Mr. Middleton's specialty was Wagner's "The Ring of the Nibelungen." He was the advisor to the music club, and most of the time was spent listening to this composition, learning about the leitmotifs related to the opera. I was in the music club for four years.

The orchestra provided me an opportunity to perform many of the important orchestral compositions in the canon, which was rare for African Americans during the time. Even today, African Americans have difficulty obtaining orchestra positions because they do not have opportunities to play in orchestras particularly. If they attend African American universities or colleges, many do not have orchestras, although some provide an orchestral experience with a community orchestra. There is also the cost of becoming a classical musician: lessons, quality instruments, and travel. For an African American to aspire to be a European classical musician requires the same kind of dedication given to sports. I had to work very hard to maintain solo chair in orchestra and concert band. Let's put a fermata on this subject.

We also had a chamber orchestra called the Symphonette, which was conducted by Dr. Constantine Johns. We performed Brandenburg Concerto no. 5 in D by Johann Sebastian Bach, "Hoe-Down from Rodeo" by Aaron Copland, and compositions by Haydn, Mozart, and Telemann. The concert band conducted by Mr. Paul Carson and Mr. Powell Middleton performed the following compositions: Fifth Symphony by Dmitri Shostakovich, Finale from the Symphony no. 4 by Peter Ilyich Tchaikovsky, and his Swan Lake Ballet.

CHAPTER SEVEN

I played basketball for West Chester for three years, one on the junior varsity and two years on the varsity. The coaches were Emil H. Mesokomer and Robert Reese. I had no plan to play basketball at West Chester, but one afternoon, I was playing a pickup game. At the time, I didn't know I was playing with some of the varsity players. I was holding my own and some. My Haddington experiences were paying off. I must have impressed the basketball manager because after the game, he asked me, "Who are you, and where do you live?" I told him, "George Allen from Philly." He told me I should try out for the team. Thinking about all my music commitments—marching band, orchestra, men's chorus, and practicing the clarinet a minimum of two hours a day—I told him I would need to think about it.

One day while walking to class, I noticed a familiar face; it was Carson Carr from Philadelphia. I had known Carson from Haddington and Mill Creek playground at Forty-Eighth and Brown Street. He played for a team called the Cobras. I told him about the half-court game and what the manager had said about trying out for the team. I asked him if he was going to try out. He said he was. I decided to go after my second love, basketball.

We became the first African Americans to play basketball at West Chester Teachers College in 1954. Making the team was the easy part for Carson and me. He was a math education major and commuting from Philadelphia every day. I was a music education major unprepared for academic challenges.

Sidebar: 10/13/2001. I made a tape of the Benedictine Monks of Santo Domingo De Silos singing Gregorian chant: Angel 4DS 55513B.

The situation was that the marching band met at the same time as basketball practice, 3:00 to 5:00 p.m. Mr. Mesikomer and Mr. Carson worked out this arrangement where I would go to marching band on Monday, Wednesday, and Friday for one hour to learn to drill for the next game, then go to basketball practice. The coach put Carson on the varsity and put me on the junior varsity. I never understood this because I was having my way with the guys on the varsity when we had to play against the varsity.

We would have won more games if Carson and I played at the same time. Later in the season after marching band, I was moved up to varsity. This caused some jealousy among some of the players. Things got pretty rough under the basket. At one of the practices, I went up for a rebound, and one of the players undercut me, and I fell on my head. They took me to the hospital. They put three clamps in my head to close the cut. I don't know why they used clamps instead of stitches, and I don't think the player was disciplined. I was not asked.

We did not have a good team. It was certainly not the quality of players I was playing against in Philadelphia. I don't think we had a winning season in the three years that I played. I would argue that we would have won more games if Carson and I played at the same time. If Carson played, I didn't play. There was one exception.

Sidebar: 10/19/2001. Attended a concert at the New Jersey Performing Arts Center in Newark, New Jersey, that featured a group consisting of Herbie Hancock on piano, Michael Brecker (from Philadelphia) on tenor, Roy Hargrove on trumpet, Brian Blade on percussion, and John Patitucci on upright bass. The concert was a celebration of the seventy-fifth birthday of Miles Davis and John Coltrane.

In my junior year, we were scheduled to play Villanova University at the Palestra, located on the University of Pennsylvania campus. The coach asked Carson and me if we knew any of the players on the Villanova team. We did because we played against some of them in the Narberth Summer League. Many of the best collegiate players played in this summer league. It was very competitive. Carson played for one of the teams, and I played for the Haddington team. After Carson and I told him what we knew about the players, he asked us how we should play the game. We made it simple. Carson would control the boards, and I would play Bill Shaffer, who was one of the top players in the country. I was also counting on them to take us lightly because they had national ranking. We worked a few offensive plays and worked on a box-and-one on defense. My job was to defend Bill Shaffer. I had to treat him like a Mozart symphony; Mozart's music is perfect.

It was an honor to play at the Palestra, and the players were excited. As the game progressed, my assumption was correct; they had taken the game lightly; with two minutes remaining in the game, we were winning by five points. I called a time-out. When I went to the huddle, to my amazement, the coach asked me why I called a time-out. I was perplexed; I couldn't believe the coach didn't know why. I finally told him that we needed to "freeze the ball." This meant they would have to foul us to get the ball. I told the team, "Do not shoot the ball." We put the ball in play, and things were going fine until for some reason one of our players shot a jumper and missed. After that, it was like a supersonic jet passing by. We lost the game. Carson played his usual fine game of controlling the boards, and I held Shaffer below his scoring average.

Sidebar: 10/20/2001. Attended a concert celebrating the seventy-fifth birthday of Jimmy Heath (from Philadelphia) at Alice Tully Hall in Lincoln Center. His brothers, Percy and Albert, also performed. The Lincoln Center Jazz Orchestra performed Jimmy's music. (Percy died on April 30, 2005, in Long Island.)

That was the only game Carson and I started. I was proud of the way Carson played. He got the rebounds, and his left-hand jumper was working. We were not afraid of Villanova because we had played against all the best players from Temple, Penn, LaSalle, and Saint Joseph's. We played Philadelphia basketball, which was defense and controlling the basketball, a.k.a. John Chaney Basketball.

When I was in high school, there was a summer band program at University of Penn. After lunch, there was recreation. I would do sixty laps in the pool and play "PIG" with Erni Beck, who played for the university.

The highlight of my basketball-playing days occurred during the summer of 1957. It was the championship game for the Narberth League, and it was a hotly contested game. The score was tied with ten seconds remaining in the game. We had the ball, and Victor Harris, our coach, called a time-out. At this point in the game, most of our starters had fouled out of the game, so I was in the game. It was an honor to be a member of this team because the team consisted of players like Guy Rogers, Wilt Chamberlain, Jay Norman, Claude Gross, John Chaney, Sonny Loyd, and Dave Riddick. So Mr. Harris set up a play where I was a decoy. I was just to stand in the corner of the court and look like I was not involved in the play until the ball was shot. At that point, I was supposed to crash the boards along with everybody else. When the ball was shot, it missed, and not being boxed out, I tapped the ball in the basket to win the game.

Sidebar: 10/26/2001. Planned to attend Philadelphia Orchestra's two o'clock performance of Mahler's Fourth Symphony and Marcus Roberts Trio that evening at Annenberg Center. Wynton's brother, Jason, plays percussion with the trio.

During my sophomore year, academically, things got a little better. This was the year I met Dr. Wright. Dr. Wright taught theory, harmony, and composition and was advisor to the jazz band. He had a comfortable style of teaching. I liked Dr. Wright because he liked jazz music and he played jazz piano on the weekends. This was important to me because the music department did not support the playing of jazz in the practice rooms. Jazz was not taught, so I had to teach myself.

Sidebar: 10/24/2001. Spent time with Wynton Marsalis and his new septet at Annenberg Center for the performing arts on the University of Pennsylvania Campus. Farrid Barron from Philadelphia played piano, but I missed the old members: Marcus Roberts, Todd Williams, Herlin Rilley, and Wycliffe Gordon.

I had Dr. Wright for three semesters. More than any of my professors, he stimulated my interest in harmony, score analysis, and composition. Now, I receive enjoyment part-writing a choral melody and putting in the figure bass in Bach chorales. Composing became very important during my teaching career, also doing arrangements for the different ensembles I conducted. I also made a habit of doing a harmonic analysis of my conducting scores. It is also important for a conductor to know the key relationships in a composition. For example: knowing the key relationships in John Coltrane's "Giant Steps" would help students learning the composition aurally. I heard Marcus Roberts tell a young piano student who had studied Bach's "Preludes and Fugues" books I and II and was beginning an interest in playing jazz music, "Take a tune that you like and listen to it for six months. After six months, then try to play it on the piano." Jazz is an aural art.

I will always remember Dr. Wright in his double-breasted suits. He was a great teacher for me because he didn't impose his knowledge of music on his students. He made learning fun. My other professors were fine, but Dr. Wright gave me the tools that started me investigating why music sounded the way it does: not only European classical music but African American classical music—jazz. This worked well with my Saturday evenings, going to the Philadelphia Orchestra concerts and listening to jazz.

Sidebar: 10/22/2001. Attended a concert honoring Quincy Jones receiving the Marian Anderson Award at the Academy of Music. Performers included the Philadelphia Orchestra, Charles Floyd and James De Preist, Grace Bumbry, Jon Faddis, and Stevie Wonder. Four members from the Philadelphia Orchestra backed up Stevie Wonder.

Chapter Eight

I spent many hours at African American Musicians Union Local 274, located on South Broad Street. The African American Musicians Local 274 played an important part in my development as a musician, rehearsing with the union concert band and going to late-night jam sessions at the union hall on South Broad Street. The visiting jazz musicians would come to the union hall after their gigs. The following is from my dissertation.

The Turner Study

Delores Diane Turner (1993) wrote a social historical study of the emergence, formation, and demise of black Local 274, American Federation of Musicians, which existed from January 2, 1935, to April 1, 1971. Turner analyzed the evolution of the Local as a social institution couched in the consciousness and collective behavior of African American musicians in Philadelphia. Relevant information in Turner's study are found in the following chapters:

1) Chapter 3, "The Founding of Local 274"

2) Chapter 4, "Growing Pain [*sic*]—The Forties and The Fifties"

3) Chapter 5, "Our Time Has Come"

The Founding of Local 274

Philadelphia African American musicians founded the Musicians' Protective Union Local 274 with a sense of racial and class consciousness.

> Union Local 591, a subsidiary of white Local 77, was the first attempt by African-Americans in Philadelphia to organize a separate union within the ranks of the AFM [American Federation of Musicians]. Although it had ceased operation by the early 1930's, Local 591, through its successes and failures, enabled the city's Black musicians [1] to gain knowledge on how to operate a union, [2] to experience some union benefits and [3] to enjoy a degree of autonomy. (p. 73)

Local 274's charter was issued on January 2, 1935. The Local's concerns during the formative years were segregation in the workplace, stabilization of union structure, membership, employment opportunities, and wages, and the Philadelphia African American musicians' collective endeavors to achieve status and power in the city's music industry (p. 75). The leadership of white Local 77 resisted the organizing of a black musicians union

(p. 96). The relationship between Local 274 and Local 77 was strained because of racial segregation (p. 128).

> In the decade that followed the thirties, Local 274 would begin to take more militant response to racial segregation [sic], which resulted in employment restrictions for Black musicians. (p. 128)

Black musicians were barred from playing in the better-paying venues. Turner's interview with James Euclid Adams, past president of Local 274, revealed conditions for local musicians during the middle to late thirties.

> You take a white band—any town—[sic] New York, Philadelphia, what not[,] [and] [t]hey could organize and go into a hotel like the [white] Adelphia Hotel. You can take a Black band that's been together for ten years—much better—[sic] all way around[,] [and] they couldn't get a gig in there. They couldn't get a job there because they were Black. They weren't hiring Black musicians like that in the hotels and finer places on Chestnut Street, Broad Street, farther down Broad Street, Wagner's Ballroom, out towards City Line, [sic] a bunch of different places. (pp. 77-78)

According to Adams, to preserve jobs for local musicians, Local 274 officials made it difficult for itinerant black bands to join the union as a group (pp. 108-109).

> Any number of bands came here and broke up because of the attitude of the union officials at that time . . . . They were acting in behalf of the local boys . . . . If you broke up and stayed here, okay. Then[,] I'll hire you individually . . . . Everybody could work but not as an organized band. (p. 108)

Despite hard times, more jobs were available for African American musicians during the mid-to-late 1930s because of the union input and the great demand for their services. Some jobs were at the finer locations. W. O. Smith, Local member, had this to say about the importance of Local 274:

> The union opened an entire new dimension for the expansion and recognition of our art . . . . We got a job at the Warwick Hotel rooftop club, a gig that in those days seemed inconceivable for black musicians. (p. 125)

The union not only had an impact on job opportunities, but it helped to develop an informal fraternity among Philadelphia African American jazz musicians (p. 125). Knowledgeable black working classes and the black elite supported the jazz musicians by their attendance at clubs, dances, and other social affairs such as teas and concerts. Turner quotes W. O. Smith.

> Most of our role models were jazz musicians . . . . In music we had the likes of Earl Hines, Fletcher Henderson, Duke Ellington, and later Count Basie. Everybody in the community knew the broadcast times and theater dates. These were the main and most exciting events in our somewhat limited lives. (p. 121)

Philadelphia musicians developed a tradition of having jam sessions, which afforded Local 274 members opportunities to perform with noted jazz musicians regularly throughout the city. John Birks "Dizzy" Gillespie expressed a common opinion among visiting jazz musicians. "The musicians used to have some baaad [*sic*] jam sessions in Philly" (p. 123).

Growing Pains the Forties and the Fifties [*sic*]

With the commercialization of "race music," white musicians found it profitable to copy the style (p. 139). Although racial discrimination persisted, some progress was made to integrate the music profession but with less than favorable results.

> The struggle to get to the top as far as the sepia [black] band is concerned has always been a doubly hard one. Prejudice, dislike, [*sic*] jealousy was the

lot of the Negro musician wherever he went [*sic*] and despite the cult of the "jam session," [*sic*] such friendliness seldom passed the doors where the session was being held. (p. 139)

On the positive side, remaining musicians during the Second World War had opportunities for employment because of enlistments and draftees (p. 154). The AFM's Music Performance Trust Fund provided additional income for Local 274 (p.158).

In September 1945, with the return of many white musicians from the war, there was an attempt by a coalition of white club owners to remove black entertainers from the bigger clubs (p. 166).

Regardless of how the patron felt [*sic*], the club-owners feel that they should take care of white entertainers first. The increasing number of sepia [African Americans] patrons who attend[ed] the places like the Swan Club, the Little Rathskeller, Ciro's, Orsatti's and Lou's Moravian . . . to see their favorites in action may have something to do with the decision to bar colored show people (p. 167).

During the 1950s, Local 274 fought to eliminate the racial discrimination and segregation in Philadelphia's music industry and to increase job opportunities for its members.

To improve employment conditions for its members, Local 274 considered: 1) having members sign I.O.U. slips with operators of cafes and clubs to secure promised engagement; 2) making sure that members got fair wages and had decent working conditions; 3) collecting overdue salaries from various cafes and clubs; 4) getting agreements signed with clubs and cafes to use union musicians; and 5) acquiring allocations from the AFM's Music Performance Trust Fund for free live concerts. (p. 191)

Although Local 77 and the recording industry controlled the production and commercialization of black music, some Local 274 members gained national visibility.

Members of Local[,] who gained prominence in the 1950s[,] included John Coltrane, "Philly Joe" Jones, Bill Doggett, Jimmy McGriff, Benny Golson, Nelson Boyd, and Elmer "Pops" Snowden. (p. 198)

The observations made by Turner (1993) are consistent with Local 274's situation during the 1940s and the 1950s.

Local 274 experienced growth and power from the 1940's [sic] through the 1950's [sic]. The union not only survived the war years but prospered into the 1950's because the general public was hungry for entertainment in Philadelphia. Local 274 also survived a major dispute in 1947[,] which resulted in a complete changeover of officials.

The union increased its stability with the purchase of a union hall in 1948. The hall provided an environment where musicians, local and out-of-town, could meet, exchange ideas, and socialize. (p. 207)

Our Time Has Come

By the mid-1940s, there were more than fifty black locals in the AFM, most of them located in southern states (p. 216). These locals, like Philadelphia, helped to perpetuate cultural identity and articulate a black perspective through their music (p. 218). Turner states that by the 1950s, black unions enjoyed their greatest autonomy and experienced growth in assets and membership. AFM's assumption was that black locals would give up their autonomy, but the Philadelphia black and white locals were the last to merge (p. 222). Local 274, due to mounting pressure from the AFM, merged with Local 77 on April 1, 1971 (p. 276). Turner details the history of AFM mergers across the country. Mergers did not improve working conditions for black musicians.

Turner's conclusion was that the majority of Philadelphia African American musicians were able to maintain their black cultural identity. However, a few of their fellow African American musicians continued to strive to measure up to Western European classical music values. They equated "success" in terms of emulating the white musicians.

Sidebar: 11/3/2001. Heard pianist Eric Lewis from Camden, New Jersey, in concert at the Painted Bride Art Center. He has something new to say; listen for him.

CHAPTER NINE

Being the first African Americans on the basketball team presented a problem for the coach. When we had away games, we would travel by car or bus. Stopping for meals, the coach would have to ask the owner if we could come inside to eat. Sometimes we did not eat with the team. Sometimes Carson and I just told him not to ask; just give us the meal money. We would use this money for bus fare back to Philadelphia if it was Saturday night and before midnight. I would get some home cooking, and Carson could go to work at Horn and Hardarts in center city. This was the year Dr. W. Glenn Killinger, legendary football coach and dean of men, told me to cut my Afro because I looked like Jesus.

As I mentioned, Carson was also my roommate. He came from a family of eight children raised by a single parent. They lived in the 600 block of June Street in a two-bedroom house in West Philadelphia. At that time, I could not imagine where everyone slept or how his mother raised them to be fine human beings like Carson. I understand it now. Carson attended West Philadelphia High School and enrolled at West Chester State Teachers College as a math education major. He and Fannie Coles from Kensington High School in Philadelphia might have been the first African American math education majors. Fannie went on to become a fine math teacher in the Philadelphia School District. She taught some of my children at Beeber Middle School.

When Carson registered at West Chester, he was at the end of the line when he was asked to go to the last table to pay his bill. Carson told them that he didn't have any money. He didn't know you needed to pay that day. That says something about the counseling we received in high school. He was told to go over and talk with a gentleman at the next table. Fortunately, it was the coach Mr. Mesokomer. He got Carson a job in the school cafeteria. With this job, weekends at Horn and Hardarts, and the post office during semester breaks, he was able to graduate in four years with a degree in math education. Carson is the dean of minority academic affairs at Albany State University in Albany, New York. Of all the frat brothers, I have the most respect to him because he did the most with less.

The routine started to get better for me, but it was very busy. In fact, I borrowed my father's car to get back and forth between West Chester and Philadelphia because of the clarinet lessons, rehearsals, and performances. One of the groups I was playing with was the Philadelphia Symphony Club Orchestra. This orchestra consisted of students from surrounding universities, colleges, conservatories, and amateurs. The purpose of the orchestra was to sight-read orchestral literature. Mr. Arthur Cohn was the conductor. He had the reputation of being one of the best sight-reading conductors. I was principal clarinetist and performed the Mozart and Nielsen concerti with the orchestra. Later I became the librarian for the orchestra. The music was borrowed from the Drinker Collection at the Free Library of Philadelphia. Later, I was the librarian for the Symphony Club Concert Band, which borrowed music from the music library of the school district. The band's conductor was Dr. Edwin Heiliaka. Like the orchestra, the band also sight-read band repertoire, but this group performed summer concerts. I was a soloist with the band on a number of occasions.

There was a memorable moment at one of the orchestra rehearsals. Mr. John Delancy, who was the principal oboist with the Philadelphia Orchestra, came to one of the rehearsals; we were sight-reading "The Barber of Seville" overture by Gioacchino Antonio Rossini. In the overture, there is a dialogue between the oboe and clarinet. After the overture was over, Mr. Delancy turned to me and said, "Nice job." I was not asked.

The summer of 1956, the family and my cousins Elwood and Gloria went to Atlantic City to spend a week with Aunt Nola. I had a part-time job working in a radio-repair shop and went to summer school for Speech II. My junior year was more of the same routine: school, concerts, rehearsals, lessons, and basketball. There was one basketball incident. We were playing LaSalle University at West Chester. Their best basketball player was Tom Gola, who was an all-American and later played for Philadelphia in the NBA. Gola was playing me, and I drove around him for a spectacular layup shot. He was embarrassed. Gola spent the rest of the game showing me why he was an all-American.

A musical activity at West Chester was the All-Star Series. These performances included Casare Siepi, Roberta Peters, Pittsburgh Symphony, Jerome Hines, Cleveland Orchestra, Jan Pierce, Walter Cassel, and the National Symphony. We also had wonderful student and faculty recitals.

The senior year was different. I got married, and I did my student teaching. I began dating Gladys Eloise Peters in the summer of 1957. My cousin Elwood and I had seen her playing the piano at a concert at First African Baptist Church, located at Sixteenth and Christian Streets in South Philadelphia. He knew I was interested in Eloise, so he said, "Why don't you ask her out for a date?" which I did. She said yes. We dated that summer. One thing led to another, and we got married on January 2, 1958. We were married for forty-seven years. My wife passed on back in January 3, 2004. We fed and nurtured thirteen children, six of our own and seven grandchildren.

My parents, many family members, and college friends were not in favor of the marriage because I had not graduated from West Chester. The thing that sold me on Eloise was I found out that she could cook. On Thanksgiving 1957, she invited me over for Thanksgiving dinner. I had never seen so much food. Eloise's family had some great cooks: her mother (Viola Peters) and Aunt Eva. I asked Eloise if she could cook like her mother and aunt. She responded, "Yes." The other reason was that Eloise was pregnant. So when we got married, I had a great cook and an expected child, and I was still a student. But that was OK with me. Somehow, I knew things would work out. It helped to have supportive parents and family. I also had to stop playing basketball for West Chester and get a job. I got a job as a dishwasher at a delicatessen in a shopping center off City Line Avenue. I was working at nights and on weekends when I didn't have rehearsals or concerts. Eloise was working for the city as a clerk. During the Christmas break, I worked at the post office. I also became a member of the Alpha Phi Alpha Fraternity, Phi Chapter—University of Pennsylvania. We moved to a one-room third-floor apartment located at Fifty-Sixth and Race Street in West Philadelphia. The apartment was cold during the winter and hot during the summer. At the time, I was doing student teaching.

During this time, student teaching was a K-12 experience. It was not specialized like they are today: lower, middle, and upper grades. My first experience was at the lower level. I taught a first grade class a calypso song called "Bossy Down." They were not responding to my well-prepared lesson plan with goals and objectives just like the method book said. I learned "Bossy Down" so well, I can sing it today. I noticed that the children were straining their necks to see me because I was like a giant to them. So I decided to get down to their level. I got down on the floor; we had a good time learning "Bossy Down" with all the related activities. My student-teacher supervisor, Ms. Dorothy Stout, entered the room. After the class, she told me that I should not get on the floor when teaching. I told her I had to get down to their level because I was so tall. She did not accept my answer. If I was interested in just a grade, I would have discontinued doing this, but I continued and received a C for student teaching. I was not asked. I found that interesting because students were learning and I was enjoying my student teaching experience. With my teaching technique, I have a habit of upsetting people who are decision makers, such as music supervisors.

The important thing I learned from student teaching was that I could teach music no matter what the ethnic or musical background was. I just loved the kids I had in front of me, and I still love them today. In the real world, a C in student teaching did not look good on my transcript. For education majors, it was the most important grade on your transcript. I accepted the C, knowing that in my mind I could teach music. Mr. Liberio told me at one of my lessons, "Never let anybody tell you that you cannot play the clarinet." No one could tell me that I could not teach music. At my senior recital, I performed the Brahms Clarinet Quintet in B Minor, Op. 115, with a wonderful student string quartet, and I prepared this masterpiece for performance. I wish I had a tape of the performance. I graduated and took my C to the Division of Music Education.

CHAPTER TEN

In Philadelphia, it was required that you had to take an examination that consisted of three parts: practical, written, and oral. It was required that you had to pass the practical in order to take the written and oral. I passed the practical, but I guess I didn't pass the written part and possibly the oral. Dr. Werson was the director of music education. Philadelphia had one of the best music education programs in the country. Seventy was the passing grade. I received a sixty-two. Later I found out that they thought I looked too young to be a teacher. The real reason was that the Division of Music Education was not passing African Americans for instrumental positions in 1958, and perhaps I did not take the exam seriously because I knew everybody in the division of music. Now, I had a degree with no job. Going to the surrounding school districts was out of the question. My goal was to teach music in Philadelphia. I was not asked.

Sidebar: 11/21-25/2001. Went to Chicago to visit my daughters, Ina and Gloria, over the Thanksgiving holiday. Ina is a middle school music educator in Evanston, Illinois, where she has a wonderful choir. Gloria is a home care visitor. I went to the Jazz Showcase on 59 W. Grand Avenue to hear one of my former students, Dwayne Burno. He is a bassist with the Roy Hargrove Quintet. Thanksgiving, I went to the Trinity United Church of Christ to celebrate "Umoja Karamu: The Ritual of the Black Family." On Saturday, went to Symphony Hall to hear the Chicago Youth Symphony Orchestra. They performed Concerto for Viola and Orchestra, Op. Posth., by Bela Bartok and the "Pines of Rome" by Ottorino Respighi. Went back that night to hear the Chicago Symphony Orchestra perform Bach's Brandenburg Concerto no. 3 in G Major; Shostakovich's Violin Concerto no. 1 in A Minor, Op. 77, Samuel Magad soloist; Kodaly's Dances of Galanta (wonderful clarinet playing by Mr. Larry Combs, principal); and Bartok's Dance Suite. Purchased two books, *Strange Fruit* by David Margolick and *And So I Sing* by Rosalyn M. Story.

I applied for a position as an activity instructor at Philadelphia State Hospital—Byberry. My duties were to play appropriate music on the wards, conduct the orchestra, play for church services, and drive the bus. I was doing music therapy, but I became bored with the routine. I met Mr. Leonard Whitmore, who is an outstanding music therapist and an Alpha brother. He taught me a lot about how to relate to the patients. I left in June 1960 and went to work for the Department of Public Welfare. My case-load area was from the 1800 to 2000 block from Washington Avenue to Christian Street. I lasted six months. My supervisor asked me to "move on." I was giving away the money too fast. All you had to do was cry. I would approve the application. That is when I first learned that some people have more stories than the library. But it was a chance to see another part of the human experience that I was not familiar with. I left in March 1961. I applied for substitute teaching and was put on the list. To keep the family going during the summer, I got a job cleaning in factories at night. This was hard and dirty work. I was not asked.

In September, my first long-term substitute appointment was at Martha Washington Elementary School, located at Forty-Forth and Aspen Street in West Philadelphia. I was assigned to a sixth grade class with my first set of twins I have had in my classes or ensembles. In my thirty years with the school district, I seem to have always taught twins. The principal was Mrs. Lola Garth. She was a dynamic principal with a vision for African American students. She had a disciplined school and concerned teaching staff. One of those was Dr. Harold Trawick, who later became principal of the school. He was also an Alpha brother. Because my goal was to teach instrumental music in the school district, I asked Mrs. Garth if I could start an orchestra at the school. She said yes. We rehearsed before school. Apparently, Mrs. Garth told Dr. Wersen what I was doing. One morning during the rehearsal, I noticed Dr. Wersen was observing me working with the students. After the rehearsal, he asked me what I was doing. I told him I was conducting an orchestra. Then he left. He didn't tell me if I was doing bad or good; he just left. We gave our Christmas program; I was transferred to the Comegys Elementary School, located at Fifty-First and Greenway Street in Southwest Philadelphia. I still see some of the Washington students today, and they remember making music.

When I walked into the main office the principal, Ms. Owens said to me, "Are you the new substitute?" and handed me the roll book, then said to me, "This class has had many substitutes. This is the worst class in the school. Do what you can with them." That's how I was introduced to this sixth grade class. In the few minutes I had before meeting the class in the yard, I looked over the students roll sheets. I noticed two things: one, most had failed cooperation, and two, absenteeism was high. In my mind, discipline became the primary objective for this class.

I met the class in the school yard. After introducing myself, I said, "Welcome to my house," then announced that we were going learn how my class was going to stand in line by size, short in the front and tall in the back. This took about fifteen minutes. Next we practiced walking up the steps quietly; that took ten minutes. Next, I assigned seats based on what I had observed, teaching them how I wanted them to stand in line and walking up the steps. Then we went over dressing room procedures. When they got back to their seats, I said to them again, "Welcome to my house." Some of my peers have said to me that the students were afraid of me because of my height, but I would have done this even if I were a midget. That's the way I approach teaching— discipline first. I had this class on a routine. We did the same activity every day for about a month. No theme and variations. We didn't go outside for recreation. We stayed in the classroom doing the basics: reading, spelling, arithmetic. With the discipline under control, the next problem was absenteeism. Some students would come to school in the morning but would not return after lunch or vice versa. Students went home for lunch. So during lunchtime, I would visit students' homes to inform whoever was home that I expected students in school all day. This worked because everybody in the block knew why I was in the block. Wherever I have taught, I'm known in the neighborhood as the music man. One day, I added to the schedule recreation from two to three on a Friday as a reward for doing good work that week. Guess what sport was the lesson?

The drills started with how to hold and pass the basketball. It was interesting listening to the class explaining to their peers about the skills they had learned. After the girls learned basketball skills, they learned about making jump rope a team sport. Two weeks later, I added music to the schedule: three to three thirty, again on a Friday. Now, this was a complete surprise to them; basketball was OK because I was tall, but when I started to sing to them, they were amazed. I was the talk of the neighborhood. I taught them "Bossy Down." You know students talk about their teachers and school.

I taught this class to sing in three parts, and they went on to represent district one at the annual music festival. One of the students in the class was excellent in math, so she took attendance every day and computed the monthly attendance. She works at a bank today. Another student had come from the south, and he had a problem reading. This was one of the students who would only come in the mornings. After I got him coming on a regular basis, we started with a primary reading book. By the end of the year, he was reading fourth grade material. Some of the students acted as tutors for him. He went on to play basketball at Bartram High School. He was a fine athlete. I believe he owns a roofing business. This is another story about this class.

One of the areas of study in sixth grade was world history. So I planned a trip to the World Affairs Council. I prepared the class for the trip. I received permission from the principal and the district, but I didn't prepare the class about the transportation to the Affairs Council, which was located in Center City. We had to use public transportation. We boarded the number 11 trolley at Fifty-Fifth and Woodland Avenue. What I didn't know was that some of the students had never ridden the subway-surface trolley to go into town. When the trolley went underground, some of the students panicked. Thank goodness for the lessons in discipline. I was able to get control of their fear. I had taken for granted that all the students had made this trip to Center City on the 11 trolley.

Sidebar: 7/19/2002. Evelyn Simms passed on in Philadelphia.

Because of my belief that mobility is important in one's educational development, I planned a trip to New York City to visit the United Nations Building and Radio City Music Hall. They had earned the trip because they worked so hard and music had caused them to come together as a group. I had taken the sixth grade class from Martha Washington on a similar trip to New York. The principal called the district office for approval;

they said no. So I asked if the home and school could sponsor the trip. She called the superintendent of school's office. They said that the home and school could not assume financial responsibility for the students in case there was an accident. I asked the parents to write letters and to bring the matter up at a home and school meeting. We went to New York. I received my first SEH-204: a discipline referral from Mr. Carl L. Fromuth. This was just before I received my first music appointment to Vare Junior High School on May 10, 1962. Mr. Fromuth did write the following in support of my appointment: "I was far from pleased by Mr. Allen's attitude throughout most of the interview. However, I do not believe that we should not delay appointing him to the position for which he qualified. I think he has learned his lesson." I did learn that lesson a little bit. So I started out as a music teacher in the School District of Philadelphia with a SEH-204. I was to receive more during my thirty years with the district. Before I continue my story, I will insert chapter 4 of my dissertation. These were some of the musicians I heard live as a young adult who helped me develop my teaching philosophy; there are only two types of music, good or bad, and human beings play music.

Sidebar: 3/16/2002. Funeral services for a Philadelphia icon, Shirley Scott, at the Triumph Baptist Church, located at Sixteenth and Wingohocking Streets. She died on March 10, 2002. Burial was at Hillside Cemetery, Roslyn, Pennsylvania, and repast was at the Philadelphia Clef Club of Jazz, located at Broad and Fitzwater Streets.

CHAPTER ELEVEN

Parts of my dissertation were interviews I did with Philadelphia African American jazz musicians.

What unique characteristics of the City of Philadelphia contributed to the development of prominent African American jazz musicians?

All the musicians interviewed were either born in Philadelphia or came to Philadelphia during infancy, except Coles, who was brought to Philadelphia at the age of twelve; and the interviewees lived in Philadelphia during the time of this study, 1945 to 1960. They were not attracted to Philadelphia; their parents were. Interviewees' comments reflect recollections from parents about what attracted them to Philadelphia and what they found when they arrived. All the interviewees stated that they lived in single row homes (Heath, P., 1994; Ballard 1995; Coles 1995; Heath, A., 1995; Heath, J., 1995; Simms 1995). This supports Hardy's (1989) conclusions that Philadelphia was a "city of homes" and that Philadelphia had "affordable housing."

Coles stated that he thought his mother came to Philadelphia because it was better educationally for him (1995). Coles attended Fitzsimmons Jr. High and majored in music at Mastbaum Vocational High School—along with jazz musicians Lee Morgan,

Red Rodney, and Bill Barron (1995). Coles stated that he left high school after one year because he had begun to play professionally (1995). Coles joined the black union—Local 274—in 1941 at the age of fifteen. Local 77 was for white musicians.

> Harry Marsh, Sr. was a member of the Greater City Elks Band and was an official in the union [Local 274], and I got a union card. It's the same thing that happened when I joined Oscar Pettiford. I didn't have a 802 card. So he got me a 802 card. I kept up my 274 card because I didn't have a desire to join 77. (Coles 1995)

According to Simms, "I guess what made them come up was for a better living and most of our family were here on my father's side" (1995).

Simms's father worked as a railroad porter in Georgia, working between Georgia and Florida, and continued to do the same work when he came to Philadelphia. He supported a family of nine children. Simms stated that her mother was home "all the time." After retirement as a railroad porter, Simms's father worked as a mechanic at the Navy Yard until his death. Simms recalled that families on both sides were in Philadelphia when the Simms family arrived in 1936 (1995). This supports Kennedy's (1969) belief that blacks came to Philadelphia because family had already settled in Philadelphia.

The Heath brothers, substantiating Kennedy (1969) and Dennis (1985), stated that economics motivated their parents to migrate to Philadelphia from Wilmington, North Carolina.

His father was the best auto mechanic in the world (Heath, P., 1994).

> My father had some skills as an automobile mechanic. He decided to move to Philadelphia and open his own business and he did very well for many years (Heath, A., 1995).

Percy Heath (1994) stated that after selling the business, economic conditions changed for the worse. Jimmy Heath also stated that "his father ran on some hard luck (Porter, interview, 1995). According to Percy Heath, there were no family members in Philadelphia when the family moved here (1994). Jimmy Heath stated that the schools and neighborhood where they lived in South Philadelphia were integrated. "Children of different races and backgrounds played together until they became teenagers (interview, Porter 1995)."

George Ballard's father worked for the Philadelphia Water Department. The Ballards had three sons: George, Monroe, and Allan. George was the oldest (1995).

Interviewees were asked to describe how they developed an interest in jazz and what projects they were working on at the present. Interviewees described their beginning interest in jazz music as first a love of music, which they heard via recordings, radio, and live performances, then later becoming influenced by the sound of an individual artist.

Although there was a keen interest in music per se, of the interviewees, only the Heaths came from a musical family. The Heaths stated that their parents were amateur musicians; the father was a clarinetist in the O. V. Catto Elk's band, and the mother was a choir member of the Nineteenth Street Baptist Church for thirty-four years (Heath, P., 1994; Heath, J., 1995; Heath, A., 1995). Albert Heath's interest in jazz music was supported because his brothers Jimmy and Percy were jazz musicians.

> I [Albert] was always interested in the drums because I have the love of rhythm and . . . because of the influence of people like Philly Joe Jones and Specks Wright and a couple of other people: guys like Harry Tucker and Charlie Rice. (1995)

Jimmy Heath recalled that his parents were friendly with a couple who owned a record store; his father had an interest in recordings by black artists. Jimmy and Percy stated that their father had the latest records.

> He [Jimmy] recalls listening to the music of Duke Ellington, Billie Holiday with Paul Whiteman, Erskine Hawkins, and Earl Hines. (Interview, Porter 1995)

> From childhood I [Percy] developed an interest
> in jazz. We played jazz music whenever it was
> available, on 78 recordings, on a Victrola. You had
> to wind the Victrola. All my life I was interested in
> jazz music. (Heath, P., 1994)

According to Jimmy Heath, he was influenced by the sound of Benny Carter, Johnny Hodges, and the big bands that performed at the Earle Theater, located in center city. His father bought him an alto saxophone when he was fourteen. Percy Heath's early musical experiences were private lessons on "keys," playing the violin at Barrett Junior High School, and singing with the family a capella gospel quartet.

> In the church, when I was 10, 11 years old, I was
> singing with my mother, grandmother, and cousin
> in a gospel quartet, called the "Family Four."
> (Heath, P., 1994)

Percy Heath stated that although he was always interested in the upright bass, he did not study the bass until 1946, after he returned from the military service as a pilot.

> Oscar Pettiford showed me how to hold the
> instrument. I was trying to learn from everybody.
> Trying to hang on to them like a leech. (Heath, P.,
> 1994)

Coles, after hearing jazz trumpeter Roy Eldridge on the radio and after appealing to his mother for an instrument, received a trumpet for Christmas with an instruction book from Sears (1995). Ballard was influenced by the American Legion Post #11 marching band and block parties on the 4600 block of Hawthorne Street, particularly the drummers. According to Ballard (1996), he studied with a Professor Coles, who came to the house.

> Professor Coles came to our house every week, I think it was on a Monday, and gave me lessons on the drums. (Ballard 1996)

Ballard continues:

> And I never forgot that, because that was the only time that I learned about "Washington Post March." All those things that I learned how to play then, and when I got in the service later in my life . . . I knew because I had learned the music back when I was a child. (1995)

Simms, a jazz vocalist, stated that her first interest in jazz was hearing jazz vocalist Sarah Vaughn's version of "If You Could See Me Now" circa 1948. According to Simms, it was also 1948 when she started listening to Philadelphia jazz musicians and being around them.

I always snuck into anybody's house who had a jukebox or a piano. My mother always had a piano . . . . and sneaking into bars that was for grownups. (1995)

Simms states that Philadelphia musicians called her Little Ella after Ella Fitzgerald (Simms 1995). Interviewees' comments substantiate Fraser's (1984) model: (1) attraction to jazz music, (2) observation, and (3) emulation of models.

All the interviewees are working musicians. Albert Heath is working on a dance project—a fusion of contemporary music and African rhythms—with schools in northern California, and he is studying world music. Even though Percy Heath stated that he was not working on any projects, only fishing, he performs with the Modern Jazz Quartet and with his brothers (1994). Jimmy Heath is the former chair of the Jazz Studies Department at Queens College, Queens, New York; and when not performing with his brothers, he performs with his own quartet and lectures around the world on jazz music. Ballard and Simms are performing with a local jazz orchestra, the Philadelphia Legends of Jazz Orchestra, which performs music from the bebop era (1995); and they both perform with several small groups around Philadelphia. Ballard stated, "Up until the last couple of years, I was running back and forth in Europe with the Clark Terry Big Band" (1995). Coles is writing a suite and putting together music for a recording session for his quintet, "The Gentlemen of Jazz" (1995).

Why was the period between 1945 and 1960 important to the development of jazz in Philadelphia?

Interviewees stated that Philadelphia jazz musicians were serious and like family (Coles 1995; Heath, A., 1995; Simms 1995; Heath, P., 1994). Simms states that Philadelphia was a mecca.

> Everybody was playing Philadelphia. Philadelphia was like New York to me because I didn't know anything about New York, you know. (1995)

According to Simms, the jazz clubs were open six days a week with matinees on Mondays and Thursdays or on Thursdays and Saturdays. About working the clubs, Ballard stated the following:

> Every night we would work, Monday through Saturday, . . . With us being the house band, we would play the first hour, from 9:00 to 10:00 and then the featured artist would come on and play after we got through. (1996)

According to Albert Heath, Philadelphia offered venues for people learning to play during this period of 1945 to 1960 (1995).

> Fred Miles used to have a place up on Mole Street. Jam sessions would go on all night across from

Spider Kelly's and it used to never close down. All the people would go over to Fred's place and man, I'm talking about everybody, Clifford Brown and everybody, all the guys would come over there, Philly Joe and Red Garland and Trane, I mean everybody. (Heath, A., 1995)

Substantiating Turner (1993), Austin (1987), and Wood (1973), Simms states, "If you wanted a good jam session, you'd go to Philly" (1995).

The jam session was an opportunity for jazz musicians to participate. Coles states the following:

You know, if you could play, you could go anywhere and play, you know, with cats that could play. And they let you play. But you know I remember times when we wouldn't let Jimmy Smith play. We wouldn't let him play because he couldn't play the blues . . . . And we would tell them, you know, it wasn't because they couldn't play, they didn't know how to play, you see. (1995)

Coles recalled that two years later, Jimmy Smith was "playing the keys off that piano."

According to Ballard, Columbia Avenue in North Philadelphia was the place for jazz musicians to develop in the late 1940s and

1950s. "During that particular era, Columbia Avenue . . . [was] the heart of all Philadelphia jazz" (Ballard 1995).

Ballard continues,

> The Zanzibar, the Northwest Club, Cafe Society, there were so many clubs in North Philadelphia and everybody would get dressed up in their finest to go down North Philadelphia to go to the various clubs where they could listen to jazz being played. (1995)

From a sociological viewpoint, Coles supports Franklin's (1975) and Hardy's (1989) statements concerning the lack of violence in Philadelphia during this period:

> Well, to begin with, at that time things weren't as bad as they are now. People seemed to have money; they could go where they wanted to. There wasn't a lot of violence. Of course, there's always violence in the community, but it wasn't like it is today. (1995)

Coles considered Jimmy Heath important during this period because he kept modern music alive in the jazz community. "It was a pure delight." According to Coles (1995), sessions were held at his house and Jimmy Heath's house (Heath, J., 1995).

It got to be like 20 to 30 guys playing from 12:00 to 12:00, you know. There wasn't a lot of responsibility because we were young players, so we didn't have that to be concerned with because we all lived at home. We didn't have any real responsibilities, only to ourselves. (Coles 1995)

During this period, Jimmy Heath formed his big band, which was modeled after the Dizzy Gillespie big band. Heath recalled some of the band members who rehearsed at his house:

alto saxophone	John Joyner
tenor saxophone	John Coltrane
	Benny Golson
	James Young
	Wilbur Campbell
baritone saxophone	Joe Adams
trumpet	Johnny Lynch
	Johnny Coles
	Bill Massey
trombone	Joe Lennard
upright bass	Percy Heath

(Interview, Porter 1995)

According to Jimmy Heath, when Howard McGhee came to town circa 1948, he took this band on the road under his own name because he had a "bigger name" than Heath. Jimmy

Heath made his first recording with McGhee's band. "Howard McGhee and Milt Jackson called him [Jimmy Heath] little bird" (interview, Porter 1995).

Percy Heath stated that the reason Philadelphia produced so many jazz musicians was because New York was close. He continues,

> It was reasonable economically for people to live in Philadelphia and be that close to New York, when one's ultimate goal was to go to New York and establish themselves. (Heath, P., 1994)

Simms indicated that she started singing professionally at about 1949 with Alex Coxes while still in high school.

> When I would have to work up in Allentown,
> I would come early in the morning; I would be
> so sleepy, and have to go to school the next day.
> (Simms 1995)

During this period, Simms recalls working with the following Philadelphia musicians: Keith Morris, Buddy Savitt, Red Rodney, Kelly Lopez, Jimmy Mobley, Calvin Powell, Jack Wright, and Coatsville Harris.

As far as groups, I learned a lot from Coatsville Harris. At the time Coatsville Harris had just left Louis Armstrong's band. (Simms 1995).

Simms continues, "In fact, we did a nice show with Sidney Bechet before he went to Paris in the '50s" (1995). Simms states that "Philadelphia has always been a training ground for jazz musicians" (1995). Like Turner (1993), Peretti (1992), Crow (1990), and Voce (1982), Simms claimed that the best jam sessions to be had in the 1950s were found in Philadelphia.

Some people say if you can make it through Philly, they say, before you go to the Apple you got it made. Regardless of who you are you had to stop into Philly. Philly was the training ground as far I was concerned. (Simms 1995)

When musicians went to New York, Simms states,

If they [musicians] needed someone else they wouldn't say let me call someone back home, they'd say man get someone out of Philadelphia. Go to the union [Local 274]. Ask anybody. (Simms 1995)

Simms stated that she got a singing job with the Erskine Hawkins Band through the black union, Local 274. According to

Simms, she met and learned from visiting musicians who worked at Pep's and the Showboat musical bars.

Ballard (1995) commented that many of the bands during the late fifties had disbanded because the musicians had moved to New York to continue their careers. That seems to point to 1960 or thereabouts as the endpoint of a particularly important era of jazz development in Philadelphia.

> The personnel had left to go to New York or California or other places where they could work more consistently and make more money. (Ballard 1995)

According to Ballard, the Philadelphia musicians that influenced him during the 1950s were Charlie Gaines, Frankie Fairfax, and Jimmy Gorman (1995).

> These guys are the ones who influenced me the most. They're the ones that I have to say I loved their work, I loved being around them, and they gave me the initiative to leave here [Philadelphia] and go to New York to try to do better for myself and pursue my career of playing the drums and music. (Ballard 1995)

In the 1940s, Ballard had worked all the jazz clubs in Philadelphia and knew it was time to go to New York; he also wanted to be with his peers (1995). Ballard worked with the Count Basie Band in the 1940s and the Duke Ellington Orchestra in the 1950s (Ballard 1995).

> One of the reasons I got the job with Duke was because his son [Mercer] recommended me because I worked with Mercer's band in New York for a couple of years in the late '40s, after I left Arnett Cobbs, Illinois Jacquet, and Eddie "Cleanhead" [Vinson]. (1995)

Ballard states, "Playing with the Duke Ellington Orchestra was the icing on the cake. It doesn't get any better than that."

Coles stated that he had a variety of jobs during his formative years in Philadelphia, jobs that required music reading skills. According to Wilkinson, you may remember, the function of music education was "the development of reading skills to perform written marching and dance band repertory" (1994, 30).

> I [Coles] played Hungarian music, Polish music; of course, Bar Mitzvahs. I played tent shows, I played Ice Capades, [and] I played full production shows and cabarets. (1995)

Coles commented that those kinds of jobs are now scarce. Unlike young players of today, Coles's formative years included working the Philadelphia jazz clubs.

Well, one of the ones that I can remember right off hand is the Paradise Club, which used to be at 16th and Fitzwater, across the street from O. V. Catto. We used to have a little three-act show in there when I was in there for a little while, then the Blue Note and the Showboat. That's where I first played with Bird [Charlie Parker], at the Showboat. And, there was Zanzibar; you know there were a lot of places—Cafe Society. On Cecil B. Moore Avenue, what used to be Columbia Avenue, they had from 9th and 20th street on Columbia Avenue one, two, three, four, five bars with live entertainment . . . . Then they had clubs out in West Philly—the 421 Club.

Then I played a garage [Wonder Bar], which they made into a nice room, where Bird used to play on Haverford Avenue. (Coles 1995)

According to Coles, in 1944 he joined a band called Slappy and the Swingsters, which was working at the Red Hill Inn in Pennsauken, New Jersey (1995).

That is where I got my real education as a trumpet player. I learned how to play for three act shows, dance theaters, and learned how to transpose

music on that job and at an early age [eighteen].
(Coles 1995)

Coles stated that he stayed in the band until 1948, then
went on the road with a band called the Adventures. This band
included John Coltrane, Red Garland, and Suggie Roses (1995).
Coles recalls his playing experiences from 1951 to 1960.

> I was in and out of New York from 1951. I came
> back home because, I think, to join Earl Bostic,
> [and] stayed with him a little over a year. I came
> home and joined the Bull Moose Jackson band.
> Came back home, and I joined Gene Ammons;
> played with him a little over a year. And then I
> just made gigs around Philadelphia for a little over
> a year. In 1955, I joined James Moody's band. In
> 1958, I went with Oscar Pettiford, then I went
> back to Moody's band. (1995)

Coles stated he also worked Club Harlem in Atlantic
City, playing full production shows in the backroom with
Philadelphian Johnny Lynch's band (1995). Coles's first big band
recording was with Gill Evans on *Out of the Cool*, recorded on
December 1960 (1995).

Albert Heath stated that the 1940s were a little before his
time, but during the 1950s, there were musicians like

Lee Morgan and Bobby Timmons, and of course Benny Golson and John Coltrane, Philly Joe and Specks Wright, Ray Bryant and the Bryant brothers. I mean I could go on and on and on naming people. And all of these people were available and accessible. I saw these people and I interacted with these people.

Even if I didn't play with them, I could go to rehearsals and hear them play. I could go to clubs and they had jam sessions and people were playing music all the time somewhere in that city [Philadelphia]. (Heath, A., 1995)

Albert Heath states that because he was known as a musician, it afforded him opportunities to move about the city and attend jam sessions. McCoy Tyner had serious jam sessions in the backroom of his mother's beauty parlor in West Philadelphia (Heath, A., 1995).

A lot of times I [Albert] couldn't play because I didn't think that I was good enough to play with some of these guys. Some of these guys were like professionals at the time and [I] would go over to listen to see what I could learn. (Heath, A. 1995)

Albert Heath commented that because of rehearsals and socializing, there was music in his house all the time.

His first professional job was with a group led by Louie Judge; he was around sixteen or seventeen. This group included Jimmy Garrison on upright bass and Freddie Simmons on piano (Heath, A., 1995).

> He [Judge] had a lot of work around the Philadelphia area, like Allentown and Darby and places like that. Basically we played in bars, and it was a great experience for us. We played a kind of rhythm and blues style, shuffle and blues music; and it was wonderful because we got a chance to play for live audiences and people enjoyed it. (Heath, A., 1995)

Albert Heath stated that he played with Coltrane in a group with Shirley Scott on organ and Bill Carney on conga drums.

> We played around Philadelphia for maybe a year, year and a half or so. Steady, working a lot, three or four times a month. You know, that's a lot locally. (Heath, A., 1995)

In 1959, Albert Heath moved to New York and joined the J. J. Johnson band, replacing Elvin Jones, who moved on to the John Coltrane Quartet.

After that, just all kinds of good things happened after I moved to New York. I got a couple of trips out here to California, and a couple of trips to Europe. I went to Brazil, I did Japan, and had my own trio at the Five Spot [New York] with Cedar Walton and Reggie Workman. We played opposite Charlie [Charles] Mingus for six months, and Thelonious Monk for six months. (Heath, A., 1995)

Most of the Philadelphia African-American musicians Albert Heath worked with were struggling artists. All the guys I've mentioned earlier were really struggling artists at the time. At the time, prominent people were people like Dizzy [Gillespie]. Dizzy was around Philadelphia and he was probably the most prominent because of his visibility and his development of this new type of playing, improvisation. He and Charlie Parker introduced it [bebop] and then they went in separate directions. (Heath, A., 1995)

Max Roach, Art Blakey, Kenny Clarke, and Philly Joe Jones were Heath's major influences from 1945 to 1960 (Heath, A., 1995).

I know Max Roach is probably tired of people saying that he's this type of a drummer, but Max Roach was the intellectual end of drumming for me; Art Blakey was the emotional, and Philly Joe was the creative . . . . Kenny Clarke was the stability. (Heath, A., 1995)

Who were the most prominent African American jazz musicians in Philadelphia between 1945 and 1960? What were their contributions to the art form?

Interviewees confirmed that John Coltrane was the most important musician during this period. According to Albert Heath, Coltrane was one of the most spiritual, loving human beings he had run across in his whole life (1995). Coltrane provided him with his first recording session.

It's the only one I've made with him. The album is called 'Coltrane' [recorded May 31, 1956] . . . . I'll never forget; I was 21 years old and we were playing in a place called Red Rooster, in Philadelphia on Market Street. Reggie Workman was playing bass with us and I think it was McCoy [Tyner] on piano. But those guys weren't chosen for the record. I made the record and I couldn't believe it. (Heath, A., 1995)

Coltrane played nonstop music because he had a short mission. Albert Heath continues, "He did it and got away; he didn't even make 40" (1995).

Simms stated that she could not foresee Coltrane becoming one of the world's great innovators of jazz music because he was never pompous about anything; he was just one of the guys (1995). Simms supports Welch's (1971) notion that Coltrane was a "quiet person."

> He didn't have to talk. You know, he did all the talking with his horn . . . . You never knew he was going to be great; it wasn't about I'm going to be big, I'm going to be great. He just grew into greatness, because he was great. (Simms 1995)

Simms continues,

> To me, when I hear people say the last couple of times that they heard him, that he wasn't playing—John always played; John always played. Not saying that he said all he had to say, but who can say it all? Nobody can say he put the horn down. He always played. (1995)

Ballard had only one opportunity (circa 1960) to work with Coltrane, and that was at the Showboat, with Harold Corbin on piano and Spanky DeBrest on bass. Ballard comments about this engagement:

> The place was crowded and jammed with people . . . . Trane got up on the bandstand and he asked me did the piano player know a lot of the tunes, because he didn't know Harold Corbin; I did. So he [Coltrane] called a tune out and counted off. I just can't recall some of the things he called in the first night, but one of the things he called was "Cherokee." We were up on that stand playing that one number for almost an hour. The people in the Showboat stood up and applauded for days. (1995)

According to Ballard, Coltrane was a magnificent gentleman and one of the greatest musicians he had ever worked with in his life (1995).

Ballard is an example of the perseverance of many of the musicians of that time.

> Doing what you love to do, and doing it until you leave here. Whenever I leave here—today, tomorrow or next week—I've played my drums all my life and I'm happiest doing that. (Ballard 1995)

Ballard (1995) stated that the following musicians made a name for Philadelphia from 1945 to 1960.

> Oh my goodness! Just to name a few of them for you: Lee Morgan; Spanky DeBrest; the Heath Brothers, Jimmy, Tootie [Albert], Percy; Jimmy Golden, one of the greatest pianist in the City of Philadelphia; Ray Bryant; and not to leave out two female great piano players in the world, Shirley Scott and Ms. Trudy Pitts; Philly Joe Jones, my dear friend, one of the greatest drummers in the world; Jimmy Hamilton, from around here, lived here for years and moved to New York; Dizzy Gillespie; Bill Doggett, one of the co-composers of "Honky-tonk"; Doc Bagby; Jimmy Gorman; these are all musicians who made a name for Philadelphia and put Philadelphia on the map. (Ballard 1995).

Coles stated there were some prominent players, which he preferred to call instead as musicians, who did not gain acclaim (1995). Coles named the following players: the Furneses brothers, Johnny Lynch, Babe Bowman, Billy Douglas, Specks Wright, Bubbles Frazier, Jimmy Goines, and Charlie Rice (1995). Coles considers Bubbles Frazier as the "baddest drummer," considering the fact that Philly Joe Jones was the most prominent (1995).

Sidebar: 12/16/2001. I received a call from a former student, Desmond Alton, violinist with the National Symphony in Washington, DC, from Hawaii.

Wanting to be serious players, according to Coles, was what made Philadelphia players unique. Primack (1979) stated that Philadelphia African American musicians had a reputation for being serious musicians (p. 16). Coles states that guys say they want to play, but they don't put in the time (1995). Coles continues,

> It wasn't Philadelphia that helped him to develop
> his style, it was the musicians. By listening to how
> they played their concepts, and how they played
> it against the melody, is what made me a player.
> (1995)

Coles's statement supports Fraser's (1984) fourth stage (emulation of models and refinement) and fifth stage (self-actualization and individual stylistic development). Coles names Clifford Brown (Wilmington, Delaware), Marcus Belgrave (Chester, Pennsylvania), Kenny Dorham, and Eddie Henderson as his favorite trumpet players. He also had thoughts about the use of the term *jazz* on the radio.

> Jazz needs to be defined by the deejay playing the
> music. You can't play all kinds of music under the

heading of jazz and call it all jazz, because it isn't. (Coles 1995)

Philadelphia's African American musicians were considered to be serious musicians. They were looked upon by their peers as teachers, and Philadelphia is viewed as a city that even today produces outstanding jazz musicians.

Simms stated the following:

> To me, you almost have to be teachers; you have to be teachers of jazz. This is what we really do need . . . . Just like Jimmy Oliver. To me, he's the daddy of all. I think he and Johnny Coles are teachers. (1995)

Albert Heath stated that Philadelphia is still producing exciting musicians. He continues,

> I can see that the tradition is still much alive and people are still developing and coming out of Philadelphia with the same intense love of jazz. (1995)

These interviews continue to substantiate why Philadelphia was unique during this period, from 1945 to 1960, and how Philadelphia's location was critical in producing world-class jazz musicians. I had the honor of knowing many of these personally and professionally.

Me & neighbor
Brooks Elementary

Overbrook High School
Orchestra C 1980 at Overbrook

Eloise, Wynton, Steve, Me

GEORGE E. ALLEN
512 N. Allison St.   Ac.
    S.A., A.A., Band, Orchestra,
Music Club, All City Band-
Orchestra, South Eastern District Band, Youth Orchestra.
    To become a music teacher is
"Red's" all-consuming ambition
. . . spends most of his time
listening to records and playing
basketball . . . homework is taboo
with him.
*It is in learning music that
many youthful hearts learn to
love.*

Overbrook High School Yearbook (1954)

Overbrook High School
Orchestra C. 1980

Me & Cousin Gloria in Virginia

Family 12/2002

Rehearsal for "Winter People Summer People" Rehearsal 1999

North Sea Jazz Festival 2009

Teaching Student at Cheyney Universiry

Me, Gloria and new Husband Kenny 2011 in Chicago

Mother, Uncle Elwood, Eloise (wife)

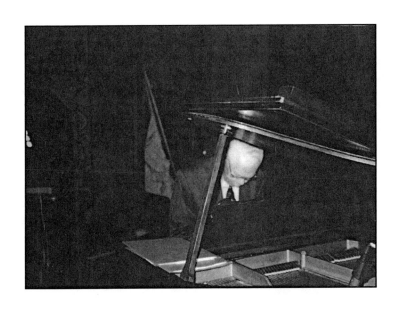

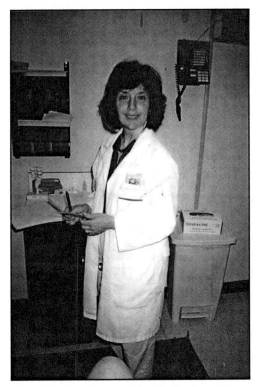

Dr. Cynthia Calbor Sezepenski Basketball Conversation

G.D. Mariah Allen
G.S. Mark Allen Jr.
from St. Mountain, GA

Early Childhood Education Students at LaRose in
Germantown for live music

NASPAAM Board Meeting

Retirement Concert from the C.C.P. Jazz Band 2001

Me making a blind pass during a West Chester game

Terrell Stafford, Micheal Clark, me, Wycliff Gordon at JALC 5/2011

Hero Awards WCU Bill Jolly, me, unknown
2009

Tony Williams & Me

Friends of The Ambassadors

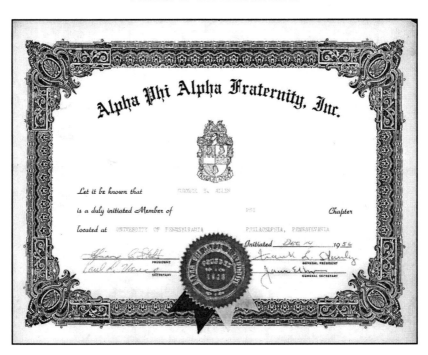

"Chilling out" at the Clifford Brown Jazz Festival in Wilmington, DE

Jeffrey Manor Civic Association Banquet
Father 3rd Left
Cousin 1st Right Anola Bishop
Cousin 4th Left Dorris Allen

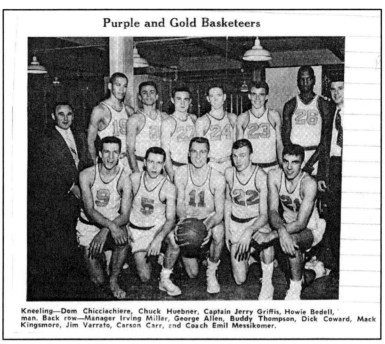

Purple and Gold Basketeers

Kneeling—Dom Chicciachiere, Chuck Huebner, Captain Jerry Griffis, Howie Bedell, man. Back row—Manager Irving Miller, George Allen, Buddy Thompson, Dick Coward, Mack Kingsmore, Jim Varrato, Carson Carr, and Coach Emil Messikomer.

West Chester State Teachers College Basketball Team

6th Annual Archdiocesan Elementary Band Festival
February 26, 1999

Pat & me with Smokey Robinson

CHAPTER TWELVE

I started teaching at Vare Junior High School in September 1962. I taught general music classes and had orchestra before school from seven forty-five to eight forty-five. The general music classes were fun for me because I could play the piano and provide interesting accompaniments for songs and rhythm exercises with drumsticks. One of the books that I used was *The Parner Songs* by Fred Beckman, who was an assistant director at the Division of Music Education. I remember him as a rather dapper dresser. I believe he owned a haberdasher store in center city. Along with teaching the curriculum, the students loved the singing and rhythm activities the best. Sometimes when I see students from the general music classes, they mention singing and rhythm activities.

One of the finest violin students at Vare Junior High was Desmond Alston. I interviewed him on February 17, 2002, in Philadelphia at the Adams Mark Hotel on City Line Avenue. Desmond was a student of mine at Vare Junior High School from 1964 to 1967. He attended Landreth Elementary School and, from Vare, attended Central High School. It was with Desmond that I started to realize that I would start teaching students who were more intelligent and talented than I. My point is that teachers can learn from their students. This remained true for my entire teaching career.

Desmond started studying the violin in the fifth grade with Hermanie Moore but went on to say, "The most influential person in my musical life was Mr. Edgar Ortenberg." Ortenberg was a Russian Jew who escaped from Paris twenty-four hours before Hitler's invasion. He was a member of the Budapest String Quartet from 1944 to 1949 and was head of the string departments at Settlement Music School, where I sent many of my students, and Temple University. Many of Ortenberg's students are in the Philadelphia Orchestra and major orchestras around the country and world. Desmond speaks about being focused.

> From the age of 8 years old, the violin was tunnel vision. Sort of envision a horse with blinders on, I couldn't see anything from the sides, the only thing I could see was straight ahead, and it was pretty much the violin. The reason why I'm sitting here . . . and give this interview is because of the violin. And the violin has been my nurturing; use all the clichés you want. I've been through many, many storms in my life and if it wasn't for the violin I really don't think I'd be sitting here right now. So I do owe a lot of who I am and a lot of my existence to the violin. (Interview, December 2002)

Desmond lived in a poor section of north Philadelphia. His mother and father were separated. I was trying to get private lessons for Desmond, but his mother could not afford them. I asked if his father could help. She said she did not think so. I asked where he lived and found out he lived around Twenty-Second and Ellsworth Street in South Philadelphia, but for some reason, she didn't know his address. Because of my habit of being known in the neighborhoods where I taught, the people knew me. After a few questions, I was able to locate Mr. Alston in one of the local bars. We had a couple of drinks, then we came up with a plan to help Desmond receive lessons at Settlement Music School. His father didn't know how well Desmond played the violin. He even started to come to some of our school concerts.

Sidebar: 12/16/2001. Went to the public opening of the new Kimmel Center of the performing Arts at Broad and Spruce Streets. Philadelphia should be proud.

When he attended Central, Settlement Music School loaned him a violin, which he kept all the way through Temple University. I wonder if Temple knew he was playing on a loaned instrument. When he was auditioning for the National Symphony, he was told to return the instrument to the owner. Sol Shoenbach, director of Settlement Music School and former first bassoonist with the Philadelphia Orchestra, arranged through a foundation for Desmond to write a letter for money to purchase a violin. Desmond states, "Actually I needed a little more than the grant and through the good graces of a very nice lady, she gave me the remaining amount." He still plays on this violin today. Desmond was concertmaster of the Temple Orchestra for three years, is presently a member of the National Symphony, and is an iron man triathlon athlete.

Another student at Vare that went on to become a musician was bassist Alphonso Johnson. One Friday afternoon, he and Vincent Hammond were taking their upright basses home for the holidays because I would not let students keep instruments in the school during holidays. Alphonso tells the following story.

> We would cut across the school yard at Childs School, at our elementary school, because he [Vincent Hammond] and I would take the same route. And we were walking together and I don't know how it started but one of my friend's winds up grabbing the neck of my bass . . . we were racing to see who could get across the school yard first . . . . My bass flipped and dropped. Well when I got home I found out that the neck had snapped off. It cracked basically. (Interview, January 2002, Long Beach, California)

I made them pay for repairs at the rate of twenty-five cents per week. They still owe the district. I make it a practice to charge students for materials and accessories even if I charged a penny.

This is important with working with intercity students. It teaches them that nothing is free.

Alphonso attended Bok Vocational School in South Philadelphia as a woodshop major. We had an excellent orchestra at Vare, but Bok didn't have one, so he played tuba, trombone, and baritone horn. He also started to play electric bass and stopped playing upright bass. During high school, he played dances and house parties, then he started to get gigs at bars during the weekends. Around 1968, I would see Alphonso playing in a group that fashioned its style like Ten Wheel Drive and Blood, Sweat and Tears. This group played service bases, colleges, and fraternity gigs. These two groups were popular groups during the '60s. He goes on to say that the day he graduated from Bok, June 1968, he kissed his mother on his way to Atlantic City to play a gig at Club Harlem, opening up for the Delfonics. After high school, he played with a group called Catalyst, made up of Odean Pope on tenor saxophone, Eddie Green on piano, Sherman Ferguson on percussion, and he on upright bass.

The next time I heard from Alphonso, sometime between 1971 and 1973, he had played with Woody Herman's big band and Chuck Magione's quartet. He had moved to Rochester, New York. In 1974, he was asked to audition for "Weather Report" by Wayne Shorter during a gig at the Academy of Music. Before he went out to Los Angeles for the audition, he called me for some advice about the audition. I told him after the audition was over, "Put the bass in the case and don't talk business with the instrument in your hand." He got the gig. His first recording with the group was "Mysterious Traveler." He stayed with the group for two years. He moved to Los Angeles and lives there today, playing and teaching. At the end of the interview, I asked him about Philadelphia's music program when he went to school.

> I wouldn't have had a career hadn't it been for that. I wouldn't have had a career. I mean it's that simple. I wouldn't think to pursue music because I couldn't afford it, you know. I was living with my mother, my younger brother and I, she was a single parent raising two boys. I remember she couldn't afford like school trips . . . that was another incentive for me to start playing, so I wouldn't be a burden on my mom when I needed extra money to do things as a teenager. (Interview, January 2002, Long Beach, California)

Some of the Vare students who helped me become a better teacher were students like Diane Puca. She had an uncle who played violin in the Philadelphia Orchestra. She teaches strings in the Philadelphia School District. Also Joe Latansie played trumpet, and Antonline Tomason played the flute. She teaches flute and performs professionally. I learned many things from them. I was not asked.

CHAPTER THIRTEEN

Like many of my students who realize their purpose early on, I realized my purpose was to teach and play music. I could not help myself from not teaching or playing music. This statement is based on the many hours of practicing the clarinet six to eight hours a day, besides the many hours listening to music by the great performers. I could have not been asked to do this. A person can be asked to practice or listen more. There is something in the "inner self" that takes over. I guess this is the process of finding oneself. For me, music education has been the process of finding the "inner self" in students. I was not asked.

Sidebar: 7/27/2002. I picked up a copy of *Teaching Genius: Dorothy DeLay and the Making of a Musician* by Barbara Lourie Sand. My son Mark and I went to see the show "Blast." He is a percussionist and tractor-trailer driver.

I guess this is why I will always be a teacher. I teach every day: whether they are my students, friends, or someone I met for the first time or some kids that happened to be nearby. It took me a while to realize that people perform music. If I could get to that "inner self," I could begin to teach music. One of the first questions I ask a new student is "Can you carry the instrument?" The question answers the question "Are you serious?" I have also learned that playing the notes or an instrument is less problematic than making a musical statement because the musical statement is a part of life. Some music educators think that music is playing the correct notes. Music became more than notes when I began to teach. Another way of putting it, "your intellect is but a speck on a sea of emotions." One of my mentors from Gratz Senior High School, Jesse Taylor, said this to me.

For music educators, it is most important to create the style of baroque, classical, romantic, and contemporary European classical music. Also, it is important to create America's classical music and jazz music than trying to sound like the Philadelphia Orchestra or the Count Basie Orchestra. Music educators seem to spend too much time learning every note in the European classical canon. As music educators, more time should be spent learning styles and interpretations. I always thought it was better to teach a variety of compositional styles. I was one of the first to introduce jazz as part of the orchestra repertoire at Vare Junior High School in 1962 and continue to do so today.

In 2000, I conducted the PMEA District 12 Band, and I chose the following program:

The Merry Wives of Windsor Otto Nicolai
                              Arr. Laurendeau
Adagio for Strings   Samuel Barber
                              Arr. Custer

Toccata	Girolamo Frescobaldi Arr. Slocum
Morceau Symphonique	Alexandre Guilmant Arr. Shephard
Valdres (Norwegian March)	Johannes Hanssen Arr. Bainum
Ghost Dance	Ouincy Hillard

    1. Incantation

    2. Dance of the Ghosts

    3. The Massacre

The Rite of Spring	Igor Stavinsky Arr. Keiser
Cajun Folk Songs	Frank Ticheli
Pop and Rock Legends: Stevie Wonder	
	Stevie Wonder Arr. Wasson
Imparito Roca	James Texidor Arr. Winter

My son George E. Allen Jr. was the trombone soloist in the Morceau Symphonique. George is a member of the US Army Band "Pershing's Own" and is a member of the Army Concert Band. The students learned to interpret the music in two and a half days. We did not rehearse the notes. They did that on their own, which they did before the rehearsals. Listening to many honors groups across the country, I am impressed with their executive skills, but I wonder if they understood the style of the music. Music is more than notes and dynamics. Singing is the beginning of teaching style. I start at the first rehearsal having the group singing a concert A or B flat on the neutral syllable la. I learned this from being around jazz musicians. They sing to other musicians if they are teaching a particular part to other musicians. A common phrase with jazz musicians is "Play it like this," and they start to sing. I have watched Wynton Marsalis do this when working with students and the Lincoln Center Jazz Orchestra.

Sidebar: 1/9-13/2002. Attended IAJE Conference in Long Beach, California. Percy Heath, McCoy Tyner, and Frank Foster were the NEA awardees for 2002. I had dinner with Jimmy and Percy Heath, Frank Foster, and Freddy Hubbard. I just sat and listened. I interviewed former students Jonnette Newton, Dwayne Burno, and Alfonse Johnson. Jonnette and Alfonse live near Long Beach, California.

One of the things that I do very well is sight-reading. The training for this began with my clarinet teacher, Mr. Liberio. He always gave me more music than I could learn in one week. I found the honors All-City groups spent too much time working on a few compositions week after week. When I was in All-City, I often wondered how much better I played my part after many weeks of rehearing the same music. I learned how to memorize my part and all the other parts as well. Today the Philadelphia district honors groups have only four or five rehearsals before the annual All-City Concert. I've been to the concerts, and the students and teachers do a fantastic job. Groups that rehearse every day or weekly should spend more time sight-reading music of different styles. I think an educational standard should be the ability to sight-read music rather than to memorize their part to the final movement of Beethoven's Fifth Symphony. Why not have the students sight-read the other three movements? Then they learn the form of a symphony and vocabulary: sonata form, exposition, development, recapitulation. Also, use the musical vocabulary. For example, I say to groups, "Start at letter A, the beginning of the exposition."

I have, on a rare occasion, had the "best" group although I had some very fine young students. It has been more important for students to perform music with correct style and interpretation. Elizabeth A. H. Green, conducting professor at the University of Michigan, commented on an adjudication at Temple University of the Overbrook Orchestra that "the orchestra was stylistically expressive . . . the orchestra performed a perfect crescendo." That was more important than having adjudicators observe that "the second clarinets are out of tune." I think not breaking the phrase at the bar line is also very important. Why do we need bar lines? Students think it means to take a breath. Ms. Green sent me an autographed copy of her book, *The Dynamic Orchestra* (1987).

Sidebar: 1/28/2002. Attended meeting at Dixon University in Harrisburg to create a virtual university for Pennsylvania University state system.

CHAPTER FOURTEEN

In May of 1965, I went to the Division of Music to apply for the senior high music exam, and the director of music, Dr. Louis Wersen, asked me why I wanted to move to high school and if I could conduct. I told him I was ready to move and I could conduct anything he could conduct. I was taken aback by the conducting question because he had seen me conduct at Vare. I also didn't want him to think that because I was black that I was not capable of conducting beyond "Mary Had a Little Lamb." During the time teaching in the district, I never wanted to be asked to move to a new position. I also told him that I wanted to go to Gratz Senior High School. I passed the exam and chose Gratz. This decision proved to be important for me because at Gratz, I began to learn the art of teaching and to become a confident music educator.

Sidebar: 2/1/2002. Attended Philadelphia Orchestra concert with my son George. He sat in his ticketed seat, and the lady next to him asked him if he was in his correct seat. After the concert, we went by train to New York to hear Mahler's third performed by the New York Philharmonic. After the concert, we had food and conversation with Joseph Alessi (principal trombonist), Julliard students, and members of the orchestra's trombone section. We missed the last R7 train out of Trenton. George's friend Ed Brown drove from Yeadon, Pensylvannia, to pick us up at 3:00 a.m.

Simon Gratz Senior High School was where I began to learn the art of teaching. Gratz had some of the finest teachers that I would meet during my thirty years in the district. I became close to three of them: Dr. Vivian Smithy, Dolores Thompson, and Jesse Taylor. They were my mentors. I started teaching at Gratz on September 1965.

At the opening faculty meeting, I was not introduced along with the other new faculty. I raised my hand and announced that I was the new music educator. The principal was Dr. Marcus Foster in his second year as principal. Dr. Foster was an innovative administrator. My roommate at West Chester did his dissertation on Dr. Foster as an administrator in Philadelphia and Oakland, California. Dr. Carr's dissertation is entitled "Marcus A. Foster: Urban Education Manager" (1981). The following is from Dr. Carr's dissertation.

After receiving his bachelor's and master's degrees, Foster began teaching sciences at Greenwood High School in Princess Anne, Maryland. After one year, he returned to Philadelphia and taught for a number of years at the Edwin M. Stanton Elementary School. He then accepted a position as a social studies collaborating teacher for District Two and auxiliary principal for the James Rhodes Elementary School. Several years later, Foster was appointed principal of the Paul Lawrence Dunbar Elementary School, where he remained for six years. He then became the principal at Octavious Catto School, a remedial disciplinary school, and remained there for three years. After a brief appointment as an educational planner assigned to the Philadelphia Board of Education, Foster became principal at Simon Gratz High School (Carr 1961).

After becoming associate superintendent for the Office of Community Affairs, in 1970, he accepted the position of superintendent of schools in Oakland, California, where he was killed.

When Dr. Foster and I came to Simon Gratz Senior High School, the school had a negative reputation. Foster states the following:

> The school, built for 2600 students forty years before was terribly overcrowded (3800); there were two shifts for students. Even with three lunch periods, students spilled out into the corridors causing a dangerous situation. The physical education facilities were the worst in the city, there was no football field—all games were played away, thus denying the school the morale that comes from inter school sports.
>
> The dropout rate was 78 percent. Or put it more directly, only one in five students entering as a

freshman graduated. Eighteen in the graduating class went to college—less than three percent. It certainly was the worst and most Potentially explosive high school situated in the city. The School Board president called it the most "short changed" school in the city. Gratz had no band, debating team, gym team, swimming team, honor society and no dances. Gratz students often viewed themselves as victims, having no control over their future, no place to go—not even down because being at Gratz, they were already at the bottom. (Carr 1981)

These were the conditions when I arrived at the school on September 1965. I was not asked.

My department head was Gertrude Garber, and the music department consisted of Carol Mitchell and Roland Bonasch. Both were very helpful in getting me started. I had a room under the stage in the auditorium where I taught band, orchestra, and theory and gave lessons. I also had help from visiting class-instrumental teachers. Students could also take lessons on Saturday mornings at music centers located throughout the city. Our center was located at Strawberry Mansion High School where I gave woodwind lessons. The only question I would ask a new student at Gratz was "Can you carry the instrument?" We started with about fifteen students, and the program grew over the years to about fifty. They became good enough to be selected by the music supervisor, Birdis Coleman, to perform at the District Four Music Festival. Mr. Coleman was the first African American instrumental supervisor in Philadelphia. He was a graduate of West Philadelphia High School and Philadelphia Musical Academy. We performed my arrangement of "MacArthur's Park." I would arrange or compose for my ensembles because I rarely had full instrumentation or the same skill levels.

Sidebar: 3/19/2002. Attended a concert at Ursinus College by Wynton's new septet: Ronald Westrey on trombone and Richard Johnson on piano. On the way back to the hotel, Wynton wanted something to drink. So we stopped at a Wawa, and during conversation with the young man at the checkout, Wynton found out that he played the alto saxophone. Wynton asked Warmdaddy [Wessell Anderson] to get his alto out of the car, and he gave an impromptu recital at 12:30 a.m. in the Wawa. It was a once-in-a-lifetime experience for the young man. I told Wynton he was the greatest music teacher on the planet. His response was "What about my trumpet playing?" He told me he has written a jazz curriculum for four to nine graders.

One of the things I learned while working with urban students is that if you can gain their trust, they will do almost anything for you. I gained their trust by being there every day on time. That they could depend on. One Friday before a Christmas holiday, we were sitting in the instrumental room, and somehow I mentioned that I needed a portable radio. Two of my students were working during holiday season at Sears. We had an unauthorized party on the last day before the holiday. I trusted them. After school, I went to put some instruments in the trunk of the car and noticed a box with a picture of a portable radio on it. I don't know how they did it because I don't remember giving my keys to anyone. The radio was top-of-the-line. I could receive stations from around the world.

One Monday, over the weekend, the instrumental room had been broken into. There were instruments missing. One of my students, Harry, said he might know where the instruments were. So we got in the car and went to the Raymond Rosen Projects on Twenty-Second Diamond Street to look for the instruments. When we got to the projects, the student said, "Wait in the car." He wanted to protect me from getting on the elevator because it was dark since there were few lights. When he returned, he had the instruments and the people who had taken the instruments. I had told the people that all I wanted were the instruments, and that was all. I told them I had students who wanted to play them and to pass the word around that we had a band at Gratz and anyone could come and check out the program. The community did not know there was a band at Gratz because very few people came to Gratz other than graduation. I never lost another instrument.

Sidebar: 3/16/2002. Funeral services for a Philadelphia icon, Shirley Scott, at the Triumph Baptist Church, located at Sixteenth and Wingohocking Streets. She died on March 10, 2002. Burial was at Hillside Cemetery, Roslyn, Pennsylvania, and repast was at the Philadelphia Clef Club of Jazz, located at Broad and Fitzwater Streets.

I also had a set of twins, the Kellys, who did all my paperwork, like excuse notes and extracurricular forms for overtime. One time, I procrastinated doing my taxes. They asked if I had the paperwork. I did. They did my taxes in school that day. When I took them home for Eloise to sign, I told her, "I did them in school."

Some of these students went on to become teachers, and two students, Katherine Richardson and Wayne Smith, became music educators. We had gotten them scholarships to Temple University. I found out that Wayne was the pinochle champion in the music lounge. I told him that if I found him in the lounge playing pinochle, I had a yardstick for him. Could one picture me walking around the music building with a yardstick? He graduated. Of all the instrumental students, Jonnette Newton was the most challenging for me. Before I talk about Jonnette, there is another story. One of the band students was a special-needs student. She would always be in the music area. One day, I asked her if she would like to play an instrument. She pointed to the bass drum. I asked her if she could carry it. She carried it. She was a walking metronome. She had perfect meter. If I changed the tempo in a piece we had played before, she would give a look of surprise. She also kept everything in the band room neat, including the band folders. We know what students can do to a music folder and sheet music. If one would come back for a second life, do come back as a music folder or sheet music.

Jonnette Newton attended Simon Gratz High School from 1965 to 1969. She should have graduated in 1968. Her mother had abandoned her seven brothers and sisters, who all had different fathers. They were raised by their grandmother. Jonnette was a student who had great academic and musical potential. She could play every instrument in the room.

One Friday, I bet her that she could not learn the break on the clarinet—A1 to B1—over the weekend. I lost. She finally settled on the tuba because the band needed one. After her Spanish teacher told her, "I will pass you on to Spanish II when you translate the textbook used in Spanish I," she did this over the weekend. Jonnette's story might sound familiar to many urban teachers.

> I was really gifted in music, but I had no way of knowing it until I got to Gratz, until Marcus Foster started the band program, and brought you on board, and you put out a notice you're looking for musicians or people who were interested in playing an instrument. I felt like I was a Pac man when I look back on it. I'm eating it up because it was something that I really loved and enjoyed. I couldn't get enough of it. So consequently, I did not go to class. I was hanging out in the music

room and I tried to play every instrument. I wanted to know everything about music I've always said music was my first love.

Jonnette continues,

> Because if it wasn't for music, I don't know what I would be doing or where I would be and to this day I try to make sure the kids are plugged into music and the arts, and all those kind of things. To me they are hooks to keep kids in school. And so, even though I'm a principal, I don't see academics as the hook to keep students. (Interview, January 2002, Long Beach, California)

Jonnette Newton is a school administrator in Long Beach, California. She continues to play the clarinet, alto and baritone saxophones, and African drums. I always visit her when I attend the International Jazz Educators Conference when it is held in Long Beach. She remembers some of the band/orchestra members. They were Thomas Darby, trumpet; Marlene Davis, alto saxophone; Marilyn Gwynne, alto saxophone and bassoon; Wayne Smith, trombone; Harry Dixon, trumpet; the Kelly twins, alto saxophone and upright bass; and Rozell Randoph, baritone horn and tenor saxophone.

Jonnette stated that all the bad kids went to Gratz. She had to go to Gratz because she could not afford the bus fare to attend another high school. Her counselor from Gillespie Middle School told her to take home economics. I asked her, "Were you a discipline problem?" She said no. She stated, "I was just a kid who didn't have home support." She was put in the clerical practice curriculum. It was teachers like Ms. Crooker and Mrs. Hammie who got her into the "upward-bound program" that prepared students for college who needed support services, and in the eleventh grade, she was put in college prep. Jonnette failed that year—too much time in the music room.

At this point, Jonnette became my favorite topic over drinks at the pub on Hunting Park Avenue on payday Fridays. One of my mentors asked me if I asked the students what they wanted. On Monday, I asked Jonnette that question. Her answer was "I want to be like you." I changed the way I related to students for the rest of my teaching career. Things got better, and she graduated, going to junior college and later to Shippensburg University of Pennsylvania. Someone said, "It takes a village to raise a child." We at times wondered if it would take a city to raise Jonnette. My mentors and I put together a group of teachers we thought would be beneficial for Jonnette.

Jonnette remembers the following stories.

> One time we were sitting on that front row in front
> of the stage where we would sit sometimes when
> we just wanted to talk. One of the things you said
> to me was that, "You know you're a pretty astute
> person." And I had no idea what the word meant,

and that was one of the first things that motivated me to go and get a dictionary and take it upon myself to find out what is the man calling me.

The other story was the following.

I think you realized that I had a lot on the ball and you used me to help give lessons . . . or you would have something to do and you would leave me with the group . . . and let me run the show a little bit. So you gave me a kind of confidence, you helped build my confidence.

One of the former Gratz students was Ronald Lee. Ronald played tenor saxophone in the Gratz Band and in a group called Force of Nature. Two other students played in the band also, Harry Dixon, trumpet, and Rozell Randolph, value trombone and tenor saxophone. I had an opportunity to work with the group when I was at Overbrook High School. They rehearsed at Warren Williams's house, located in Fairmount Park near the Strawberry Mansion section of Philadelphia. I went on tours with them to Connecticut and Virginia. The other members of the group were Ronald James, lead guitar/vocals; Donald Harmon, rhythm guitar/vocals; Warren Patterson, trombone/vocals; Cleveland Brunson, congas/timbales/vocals; Gerald James, drums; and Brian Evans, lead vocals. In 1974, they recorded "Force of Nature" at CBS Inc.

CHAPTER FIFTEEN

Chapter 15 is about my educational and musical time at Overbrook High School. In May 1972, I applied for the position of department head of Art and Music Magnet Program at Overbrook Senior High School. The results of the exam placed me second. I continued to teach at Gratz Senior High School. During the course of the school year, the chair of the Music Department at Overbrook died, and I was in line to accept the position. I was scheduled to start in February, but the school district was on strike. The strike lasted about eight weeks, not including three weeks in September.

Out of 11,300 teachers, 3,340 went to work. Out of 289 schools, 225 were open. Out of 285,000 students, 98,447 were in attendance. I was one of the 3,340 teachers who went to work after staying out for about six weeks. Having six children at that time, I decided to go back to work. In fact, I started my career at Overbrook as a scapegoat. Needless to say, there were many days of animosity. It was a very difficult period in my life. I was not asked. My main motivation was my family and concerns for the students. I knew the conditions at Overbrook because my daughter Ina was a music magnet student. I was concerned about the attitude of the students. Teachers were telling them "how good they were." They were talented, but I was concerned that talent would not get them into the best music and art schools. I also wanted students to be aware that there was more to life than talent.

One of the first things I did was to institute three rules for the department. The first rule was you had to bring your head to school every day. I would say to the students, "If you are not sure, ask yourself, do I have my head with me?" I wanted students to be in the correct state of mind for learning not only music but also how to read, write, and compute. The second rule was you had to bring a number two pencil to school every day. The number two pencil is a world standard if you are an artist or musician. That also meant that in order to do a job, one needed to have the correct materials. I used the number two pencil as an analogy for "Bring your books to school every day and take them home every day in order to be successful in life." The third rule was "You must always have manners."

I knew that in order to have a successful program, I would have to bring in people who had already done and accomplished what my students were attempting to accomplish. One of the things I wanted to assure them was when we had guest, our house was in order. We made sure that students did not talk when someone was talking and they were paying attention. At the end of a presentation, a student had to say thank you to our guest. Many of our guests commented that they would like to come back. I see these rules when I attend presentations at the Girard Academic Music Program. Dr. Jack Carr is the director. I can see him now with a student who didn't understand the rules. It would not sound like "Brahms Lullaby." It would sound more like "The Right of Spring."

I didn't know it at the time when I was crossing the picket line that Overbrook was one of the union strongholds in the school district. Many of the union leaders had come from Overbrook. I quickly learned. Not only did I have difficulty with some faculty, but I also had problems with the principal, Leroy Layton. There were some faculty who understood and accepted the fact that I had crossed the line. It seemed the principal and I could not get together in terms of what the program was going to be for the students. It reached the point where I felt I needed a meeting with Mr. Layton. My mother always told me that when I needed to talk to someone who was sitting down, "do not stand," because I am six four.

At this meeting, I forgot my mother's rule. I stood and said to Mr. Layton, "There are some people who I allow to see my balls, and there are some special people who I allow to touch my b—, but I don't allow anyone to squeeze them." I needed to tell him I was a man first. After this meeting, we went on to do great things for the art and music students. He was very supportive of the art and music magnet program. Some of those things will follow.

One of the things I found out about Mr. Layton was that he liked classical music. He attended the Philadelphia Orchestra concerts. One of his favorite composers was Johannes Brahms. Once we had a meeting of the minds, I programmed the final movement of Brahms's First Symphony. It was a wonderful marriage because Brahms was at the time one of my favorite composers. I memorized the score. I learned to understand Mr. Layton's position; he was Jewish. The cabinet was largely Jewish, and they were his friends. They had been at the school for many years. Some were there when I graduated in 1954.

One of my mentors told me, "Don't get involved with adult things. Stay close to the students." I thought of that when I was crossing the picket line. I did not want students to go down the path they were going. Teachers were telling them they were good. I knew they were good, but I wanted them to be better. The idea of good was maybe not acceptable in the finer music schools. I learned that when I applied for Temple's music program. I had the music, but I did not have reading, writing, and computing skills.

Before I started teaching at Overbrook, I was asked by the director of student activities, Henry Varlack, to take over the Philadelphia Community College Jazz Band, which lasted for twenty-five years. We rehearsed from seven to nine every Wednesday night. The rehearsal became a tradition for Philadelphia jazz musicians to sit in and work on their sight-reading. I don't know a Philadelphia jazz musician that didn't sit in these rehearsals. We would sight-read music at every rehearsal. We did prepare for concerts, but our main emphasis was on sight-reading. I was an excellent sight-reader. I learned this from my clarinet teacher, Mr. Liberio. He would give more than I could learn in a week, so part of the lessons was sight-reading. We also had a sight-reading concert band, which met on Saturday mornings from ten to twelve. I would borrow the music from the division of music.

Clayton White was the music department chair. At the winter and spring concerts, he would hire professional musicians to accompany the choir. One year, I conducted Samuel Barber's "Adagio for Strings." The conductor of the group said to me that I had a nice beat. I was about something else—style. I was not asked.

Not only did I teach the jazz band, periodically I taught courses in the music department. They were music of black Americans, music theory, music history, and piano. When I retired from the college, I formed an alumni jazz band, and we had a wonderful concert at the college. Members of this band included saxophones: Julian Pressley, Louis Taylor, Robert Landham, and Terry Lawson; trombones: George Allen Jr., Gregory Roberts Sr., Wayne Smith, and Ronald LaMar; trumpets: David Gaines, Jacob Lane, Duane Eubanks, Ricardo Jackson, and Jason Holloway; and rhythm section: Donald Robinson (piano), Clifton Kellem (upright bass), Mark Allen Sr. (percussion), Harry "Butch" Reed (drums), and Ronald Horne (guitar). The CCP jazz band also performed. The members of this band included saxophones: Harry Mobley, Umar A. Hakim, Derrick El, Daryll Banks, Taylor Hightower, Art Loeb, and Michael Shabazz; trombones: Wayne Smith, Philip Torrez, and Ebenezer Welsh; trumpets: Jason Holloway, James Puvis, and Steve Baylock; and rhythm section: Andrew Maleson (piano), Kevin Miles Gardner (electric bass), Lamar Prince and Pete Gaudioso (drums), Robert

Richardson (guitar), and Tanya Howard (vocals). We had a good time making music. My assistant was Wayne Smith, whom I had taught at Gratz Senior High School. He is presently directing the jazz band and doing a wonderful job.

One time, the band was on tour from Philadelphia to North Carolina, ending in New York before returning to Philadelphia. One of the band members decided he wanted to get off the bus on Interstate 95. This was not a rest stop. We finally convinced him that it was not a good idea. How we got him back on the bus. I could not remember reading about this kind of situation in the music method books. I was not asked.

We had a talented student activity department at the college. We had Roscoe Gill and Donald Dumpson for choir, German Wilson for drama, and Faith Snow for dance. Debbie Powell and Bernice Burley kept everybody together. They were the secretaries for the student activities department. After Henry Varlack, Gale Harkins became the chair of the department. Two others followed after Gail.

One program the division of music education had was a Saturday-morning instrumental program. The program provided individual instruction and rehearsal for All-City ensembles. I began working with the junior high All-City ensembles at a girls high school at Broad and Olney Streets. Later I worked with the All-City senior high groups at the old Northeast High School at Eighth and Lehigh Avenue every Tuesday night. When I went to Overbrook, I knew many of the students who were attending Overbrook and knew what their playing capabilities were. I developed a relationship with the Settlement Music School and Mrs. Miles, who was a longtime administrator at the Queen Street branch. She looked out for my students. When Mrs. Miles called me about one of my students who had a problem, it was taken care of that day.

After a lot of salesmanship, lessons at Settlement became part of the music magnet program. I wanted Settlement for my students because the program supported not only the music part of the program but also the discipline part of my program: the three rules. Many of the students had begun instruction with a class instrumental teacher who might not have been a specialist on the instrument the students were learning. For example, my main instruments were clarinet and saxophone, but I might need to teach flute, oboe, or bassoon, which I could do but only so far. For the level I wanted my students to achieve, they needed private instruction. I knew lessons at Settlement worked because three of my children, Ina, George Jr., and Mark, attended Settlement. Ina and George Jr. have careers in music. Ina is an outstanding music educator in Evanston, Illinois. George Jr. is a first-call trombonist in the Baltimore-Washington area after retiring from the United States Army band in Washington, "Pershing's Own." Mark is mentoring his son, Mark Jr., who is studying the clarinet in the Atlanta Symphony Leadership Program for minority students. I made a deal with Mark Jr. When he learned the Mozart Clarinet Concerto, I would give him my set of clarinets. He has my set. I was not asked.

Around 1985, I attended a lecture at Temple University given by Dr. Edwin E. Gordon on music learning theory. I became Gordonized. I took every course he taught at Temple, which for me was very challenging. I attended his workshops throughout the country. Dr. Gordon would give multiple choice exams that were the most difficult I have ever taken. I would be the last person to leave the exam. I never received higher than a B. I also was a founding board member of the Gordon Institute for Music Learning. Some of these members included Dr. Roger Dean, Dr. Beth Bolton, Dr. Richard F. Grunow, Dr. Christopher Azzara, Dr. Cynthia Crump Taggart, Robert Harper, Mitchell Haverly, Ellen Deacon, Dick McCrystal, Dr. James Gordon, Dr. Sally Weaver, and Harry Semerjian. One of the places we would have board retreats was Ocean Glove, New Jersey. The following are a few random notes taken at a summer seminar in 1986 at Temple University's Sugarloaf Conference Center, where I met most of these board members. I learned by listening to these great minds. I spent thirty years teaching in Philadelphia. My administrators would ask me, "How did you do that?" and I would say, "I don't know. I just did it." I would not tell them I was hanging out with some of the best minds in music education.

The purpose of the following is to give the reader some information about music learning theory.

Music Learning Theory

Learning theory is based on how children learn, when they learn, and what they learn.

Audiate means to perform music that is not physically present.

Teachers must have good teaching techniques and be excellent musicians.

Technique is how it is done.

Stages of Audiation

1. Hearing sound, "blast of sound"
2. Organizing patterns
3. Creating syntax
4. Comparing
5. Predicting

Notation helps you to remember what you already know. There is no presence.

Types of Audiation

1. Listening
2. Reading
3. Writing
4. Recalling
5. Creating and improvising
6. Creating and composing

Method versus Technique

1. Teachers have been taught technique, not method (i.e., how to do it).
2. *Method* is the when, what, and why at the appropriate time; this leads to curriculum.
3. We should learn music the way we learn language.
4. We must start audiation in the early grades.
5. Students educate themselves—we teach. "One is motivated to learn because he learns."
6. Meaning comes through prediction.

Learning: Discrimination/Inference

Discrimination—Teach by rote instruction. Teacher does the teaching; student does the learning of the familiar. It is readiness for inference learning; teacher tells.

Inference—Students teach themselves; without discriminate learning, you cannot make inferences. Teacher cannot teach learning.

Appreciation versus Understanding

1. Understanding does not guarantee appreciation.
2. Music learning theory can lead to musical understanding.

Levels of Discrimination Learning

Aural/Oral

Aural—hearing/perception

Oral—performing/sensation

1. Singing
2. Movement

Child must be exposed to many patterns and does not need to understand them.

From birth to three years, a child cannot remember.

Scales and single notes are not important for audiation.

Lowest level of discriminate learning is the most important.

Children need many listening and speaking experiences and must hear and perform lots of music.

Children must go through a readiness stage or language growth.

Teach many patterns; you don't have to sing everything you hear, and you don't have to hear everything you sing.

Don't use syllables at this level; use "bum."

Never mix melody with rhythm in the same class period.

Use same keyality with melodic patterns.

Verbal Association—Discrimination Learning

1. Do not require students to read tonal or rhythm patterns; purpose is to develop the vocabulary for audiation.

2. Do not teach tonal patterns and rhythm patterns during the same class.
3. A sign is an indication whereas a symbol "do" is a representation.
4. We learn symbols in order to audiate.
5. The syllables are a vehicle for audiation.
6. Syntax.

    a. Rhythm
        1. Macro and micro beats
        2. Melodic rhythm is the division and elongation of macro and micro beats.
    b. Symbols
        1. Macro beats—"du"
        2. Micro beats—"du-de" for duple meter "du-da-de" for triple meter
    c. Tonal
        1. Major—minor
        2. Tonic—dominant
    d. Symbols
        1. Fa-sol syllables

7. Syllable names help to store more patterns.
8. Verbal association gives logic to aural/oral and meaning to notation.
9. Only add symbols to familiar patterns.
10. Don't sing diatonic patterns because they don't force audiation.

11. Start with rhythm patterns.

12. Never audiate between intervals; don't break a pattern.

13. Use moveable "do."

Partial Synthesis (Remember to tell, not ask)

1. When you are listening to familiar patterns and determining meter or tonality, you are synthesizing.

2. Tell students what they are hearing.

3. There are parallels at partial synthesis.

   a. Major—minor tonality
   b. Duple—triple meter

4. This is an opportunity to give meaning to a lot of patterns.

   Hierarchy of Musical Vocabularies
   Listening
   Singing or movement
   Reading
   Writing

Subjective tonality or meter is when we don't agree on a combination of tonalities or meters.

Objective tonality or meter is when we do agree—"it is."

Symbolic Association (Reading—Writing)

1. Do reading first, writing second.
2. Bring audiation to symbolic association.
3. Familiar patterns can be in unfamiliar order.
4. Do not write a syllable on the board.
5. You must have readiness at the previous three levels.
6. After performing a pattern, put the pattern on the board.
7. Don't teach anything that is not needed now.

Composite Synthesis (Reading—Writing)

1. It is the highest level of discrimination learning.
2. No writing or reading should be done until this level.
3. This level is the ability to read music and know what the meter and tonality are.
4. Do not teach music theory. Don't write on the board what it is. This is still discriminate learning.
5. This is reading and writing with comprehension.

Inference Learning
Generalization (Aural/Oral—Verbal—Symbolic)

1. This is the ability to make an inference at the aural/oral, verbal, and symbolic level of learning from the unfamiliar.

2. You should not be teaching rote at this level. Keep asking students to help themselves.

3. Generalization is readiness for sight-reading and writing.

4. You must have one unfamiliar pattern with familiar patterns.

5. Ask, "Are these patterns the same or different?"

Example:
Melodic Major do-mi-do Minor la-do-me
Rhythm Duple Triple

6. Don't assume that students can't do something because you cannot do it.

7. Readiness is the ability to hear musical sound, to put symbols to it, and to perform it (i.e., sight-reading or writing).

Technique is the *how*.
Method is the *what*.
Curriculum is the *when*.

Creativity/Improvisation (Aural/Oral—Verbal—Symbolic)

1. Creativity—less restrictions.

2. Improvisation—more restrictions.

3. In order to create or improvise to any extent, discrimination learning is required.

Theoretical Understanding

It is an explanation of what students already know.

1. Cadences
2. Line and spaces
3. Keys
4. Meter
5. Duple and triple meter
6. Half and whole steps
7. Four-part writing
8. Intervals

I started using MLT (music learning theory) in my music classes around 1986. One of the things I liked about MLT was the hand signals: no talking. The other thing I liked was everything was performed by teacher and students. Patterns were divided into easy, moderate, and difficult. Before I started MLT, I tested the students for musical aptitude. Dr. Gordon had developed a test for musical aptitude called the musical aptitude profile. This test was given to all music magnet students. When a student was asked to perform a pattern, I knew what the student's music aptitude was. As a group, students performed all the patterns. Individually, students performed patterns according to their aptitude: low aptitude would perform the low patterns, moderate aptitude would perform moderate patterns, and high aptitude would perform high patterns. Sometimes I would ask a student to perform a pattern higher than their tested aptitude.

I found that some students did not do well on test day. Those students would be retested, and most of the time, they did better. For me, it was the best way to teach music.

In harmony class, I would audiate a cantus firmus, then put it on the board. Students knew I was audiating. I only used tonic, dominate, and subdominate harmonies in major and minor tonalities. Students knew major tonic was do-mi-sol, dominate was sol-ti-re, and subdominate was fa-la-do. After students filled in the alto, tenor, and bass, I would put the harmonization on the board. Students would perform this harmonization after making needed corrections. Students knew their voice parts. The only thing I would perform was where the resting tone was, and we did use sol-fa syllables.

I only used "do" signatures up to four flats and four sharps. I thought it was impractical to go higher. An outcome of MLT is that students become better musicians. I was able to show them in band, orchestra, and choir that they had performed the patterns in class. Often we do not transfer what is learned in theory class to our performing groups. Often I would stop the ensemble and say "That was duple major" or "That was Dorian mode" and go on with the rehearsal. Later in the rehearsal, I would go into inference mode, but I would tell them what it is first if it was a new skill, I would repeat it in discrimination mode. A good teaching technique is telling the students, "This is not important, so you will need to remember this." It works. Did you ever conduct a rehearsal and didn't talk? I would softly say to the ensemble, "I have a bad cold today, can't talk." Try it. As music educators, we talk too much anyhow. We really do.

In 1987, I met with a group of parents at Overbrook and gave a short talk on how to recognize and develop your child's musical potential.

Every child will not grow up to be a famous musician like Marian Anderson, Miles Davis, or Stevie Wonder, but every child has the potential to develop an understanding and appreciation for music in its many forms and styles.

Music aptitude should be identified and developed because it can help young children get off to a good start in music and life in a number of ways. Music helps them to comprehend and value the qualitative aspects of life. Music helps them understand themselves, others, and fundamental human issues. Music helps to stimulate their imagination.

The hard work and discipline involved in reaching one's musical potential can spill over into other academic areas. Through music, students can develop skills in reading, practicing, listening, and involvement with long-range planning. They also learn about group dynamics and processes since most students who participate in music take part at a group level, whether as part of a jazz quartet or symphony orchestra. The student learns how to interpret and evaluate musical works as well as study historical and cultural roots of music. This knowledge can be used throughout their educational experiences.

Before children learn to speak, they produce babble, those "goo-goos" and "da-das" that make Mom and Dad proud.

Likewise, there is musical babble, the sounds a young child makes before he or she develops tonality and meter. This babble is monotone and without meter, but with the correct instruction, this can turn into meaningful understanding and appreciation.

Studies have shown that the average child enters first grade with a vocabulary of about two thousand words. By about twelfth grade, many additional thousands of words have been added.

What we would like to do in music is to prepare youngsters so that when they enter school, they also have a musical vocabulary of musical sounds and patterns. ·

What do parents look for in terms of musical aptitude?
Here are a few clues:

- Does the child have a general curiosity about things?
- Can they stay on task until completion?
- What does the child do when they hear music? Do they move in tempo in a consistent beat (i.e., moving arms and legs or tapping a table)?
- Does the child exhibit spontaneous musical movement or sing without prompting of an adult?
- Does the child have pitch discrimination? For example, does the child simply bang on a piano, or does the child seem able to discriminate between high and low notes?

These are just some of the indications that a child might have musical potential. These behaviors should be encouraged and reinforced by parents when they see or hear them.

Another way to be supportive of a child's musical abilities is to expose the child to a wide variety of music. Keep that radio dial moving. Children should hear classical, gospel, jazz, opera, rhythm and blues, rock and roll, and the top forty. Buy a diverse selection of recordings and tapes for your child to hear.

Informal instruction should take place as often as possible to encourage children to respond spontaneously to music. Much of this instruction takes place in the form of games. Make up songs with your child. Create new dances to music. Sing to your child regularly. Do not use words when singing. Use "bum" or neutral syllables. In fact, a simple "la-la-la" will suffice. The important thing is that the child is exposed to and performing music.

Formal instruction is the next step. When that should begin will be different for every child, but it should be after the child is out of babble. I recommend group rather than private instruction for beginning students.

There are two excellent youth music programs in the Philadelphia area: the Temple University Preparatory Music Program, which meet on Saturday mornings during the academic year, and the Settlement Music School Early Children's Program. Temple's program starts with children starting at age one. Dr. Gordon is investigating music learning with unborn children. Music education can and should be a part of one's life. There are fine music programs in many schools. Talk to your child's music teacher and become involved with this important part of your child's creative development.

I find this even today in my teaching at Cheyney University of Pennsylvania from 1997 to 2008 in my music history classes. I sing to them, and I have them respond back. When listening to a recording, I have them keep the macro beat with the heels of their feet, not the toes. I tell them that when they attend the next rock concert to look at the musician's feet and when they are dancing to notice what their feet are doing. I demonstrate so they know what to look for. I don't have students sit there and listen to recordings. I divided my classes into groups, and each group had a theme song. I know that in order for students to really know, they need to perform the music. I don't get much rebellion. They do it because they see me perform and "This is my house." Many of Dr. Gordon's writings are published by GIA Publications Inc.

One of the programs I added to the music magnet program was music history. We used the Prentice Hall History of Music series. I wanted music magnet students to know why the different historical periods sounded the way they did and also to have a historical background. One of the things I did in my theory and harmony class was I required all my students to compose original compositions. The only rule was that they could not compose at the piano. They had to compose music based on what they could audiate. Some could only audiate quarter notes or one note or small motives. That is where most students started. Once they became familiar with and accepted the fact that they had these musical patterns in their heads and were able to put them down on manuscript paper, they became better. In the winter and spring, we would have a recital of new compositions. The reason I did this was it made them better musicians. I further developed the idea with a group of high-aptitude music magnet students. I wrote a proposal to fund a project for students to compose original compositions in four musical styles: baroque, classical, romantic, and contemporary. We worked very closely with Professor Larry Nelson, professor of composition at West Chester University, and other visiting composers. Through this project, I met Peter A. Benoliel, a benefactor of the arts. We became friends. I introduced him and his wife to Wynton Marsalis at one of his concerts.

One of the performing groups at Overbrook was the Overbrook Singers. They were a gospel group and one of the first to be organized in a Philadelphia public high school. The group was started by a music teacher who was married to the great jazz organist, Jimmy Smith, from Norristown, Pennsylvania. When I came to Overbrook, I became their sponsor. On February 26, 2002, I interviewed Stacy Walker at her home outside of Harrisburg, Pennsylvania. She was a member and officer of the Overbrook Singers, concert choir, and All-City Choir and was a music magnet student. The day she auditioned for the music magnet program, Stevie Wonder was a guest at Overbrook. The Overbrook Singers performed for him. She auditioned for the Overbrook Singers that day because she was impressed by how well they sounded. Many people did not know that many members of the group were music magnet students. They were taking private lessons. They rehearsed at 7:00 to 8:00 a.m. every school day. They had rules. You had to be on time, and you could not miss engagements, or you were out of the group. Some of the student conductors were Harry Benson, Elisabeth Frazier, and Robert Smith.

One year, they participated in the New York chapter of the National Black Music Caucus Gospel Competition. I have been a judge for many years. The competition was organized by Dr. Camille Taylor, a music supervisor in the New York School District. We came in second place, but people thought we were the best that night. We needed security to escort the group to the bus. There was damage to the tires. The bus company sent a replacement bus, and we were able to get back to Philadelphia with our second-place trophy.

We also went on a tour during one of the Christmas breaks to Pittsburgh, Pennsylvania; Detroit, Michigan; Columbus, Ohio; and Chicago, Illinois. On our way to Chicago, we drove through a blizzard. They performed for Kwanza at Oprah Winfrey's church. Under my supervision, the student leaders made all the arrangements. The only thing that I really supervised was the hotel-sleeping arrangements. I was not asked. They raised all the money except for $2,000.00 because the bus they wanted had to have a stereo system and a television. I called Wynton and told him about the situation. He said, "Have Stacy call me," and she would have to ask him for the money. Stacy states from the 2002 interview,

I was really afraid. But you called him and said, "There you go." And I spoke to him, and he pretty much knew why I was calling. I think that was you who had talked to him prior. But, he still Made me ask for the money, you know, he didn't offer it. He Said, "I hear you're having some difficulties, and I told him, "Yes, we're having a financial problem." He said, "well, what's the problem?" I said "well we need to obtain a bigger bus than the one we can afford and we're almost $2000.00 shy. And I don't know where to get the money from." And he said, "I know where you can get the money from, all you need to do is ask." He said, "it's not as hard as you think, just let it roll off your tongue." And I said, "Mr. Marsalis, would you donate the money to us?" He said, "sure, now was that hard?" And I said "no." He said, "I told you." You know, he mentioned, He remembered me singing to him when he was at Overbrook. He said someone that has a voice that beautiful, you can get anything you want from him. I put a big smile on my face. He gave us more than we needed, he gave us $3,000.00.

This is classic Wynton; he is the greatest teacher I know. He teaches 365 days a year. Can you hear him telling a female, "You have a voice that's beautiful, and it can get anything you want from me"?

Sidebar: 12/20/2011. Attended Overbrook's Annual Winter Concert, and very few Overbrook students performed. I did hear a wonderful flutist, Marie Wells. I left depressed.

On November 6, 1987, I presented a paper at the Berlin Jazzfest in West Berlin, Germany. The paper was called "John William Coltrane, the Philadelphia Connection." At the time, I was the director of education for TranStop Institute Inc. We created the Change of the Century Orchestra to create the recording "Africa/Brass" (1961, Impulse 6). Philadelphia musicians included in the group were Oden Pope, tenor saxophone; Bayard Lancaster, flute and alto saxophone; Dave Burrell, piano; Karn Jemal, vibraphone; and Brown, bass. The group was conducted by Angelo Frescarini.

John William Coltrane was born in a second-floor apartment at the corner of Hamlet Street and Bridges Avenue in Hamlet, North Carolina.

There on September 23, 1926—the equinox; the day when the sun crosses the equator and when night and day are of equal length throughout the earth; the day between summer and fall, between Virgo and Libra; with a rising sign between Pisces and Aquarius and a moon in Aries—John William Coltrane was born with the help of a midwife (Simpkins 1975).

After two months, his family moved to High Point, North Carolina, where he received his early education. Coltrane came to Philadelphia in 1944, and at this time, he was playing clarinet and alto saxophone. His real formal music instruction and social education began when he came to the City of Brotherly Love. The Ornstein School of Music started his musical training, and he later won a scholarship in performance and composition at the Granoff Studios, which became the College of Performing Arts and then to its present name, the University of the Arts. His saxophone teacher was Mike Querro, the premier woodwind teacher in Philadelphia. Philadelphia was also important because it was Coltrane's opportunity to meet musicians who were actually involved in the vocation. Some of them were tenor players: Jimmy Heath, Bill Barron, Jimmy Oliver, John Glen, and Benny Golson. Coltrane changed to tenor in 1947. Charlie Parker helped to influence the change along with the aforementioned tenor players. Composition influences were Calvin Massy and Jimmy Barron.

Coltrane's religious influences include the following:

1. Charles Greenles, Cousin Mary's first husband, introduced Coltrane to Islam.
2. Musicians noticed the change in 1957, but some were aware of the change in the late forties.
3. First wife, Naima, whom Coltrane married on October 3, 1955, right after joining the Miles Davis band.

However, Coltrane never converted to Islam although it had a profound, positive effect on him.

Many of the clubs where Coltrane performed before joining Miles's band were located in North Philadelphia on Columbia

Avenue, now named Celia B. Moore Avenue. They were Zanzibar, the Web, DownBeat, Café Society, and the Crystal Bar. I remember seeing John as a youngster performing at the 421 Club in West Philadelphia. These clubs were training places for many Philadelphia musicians, including me as a listener and student.

Coltrane's drug and alcohol abuse started in Philadelphia during late '40s along with Jimmy Heath, who later went to prison. Heath later helped Coltrane to beat the drug cycle in 1957. Others who helped Coltrane were Clifford Brown, Reggie Workman, and McCoy Tyner. The frustrations that Coltrane experienced were not unique.

Of all the Philadelphia musicians who influenced Coltrane, two stand out. They influenced all his apprenticeship years in Philadelphia. They were Jimmy Heath and Calvin Massey. Coltrane said the following of Heath:

> Jimmy Heath, who, besides being a wonderful saxophonist understood a lot about musical construction. I joined his group in Philadelphia in 1948. We were very much alike in our feelings, phrasing, and a whole lot of ways. Our musical appetites were the same. We used to practice together and he would write out some of the things we were interested in. We would take things from records and digest them. In this way we learned about the techniques being used by writer and arrangers.

Coltrane said the following about Massey:

> Another friend and I learned together in
> Philadelphia Calvin Massey, a trumpeter and
> composer . . . His musical ideas and mine often
> run parallel, and we've collaborated quite often.
> We helped each other advance musically by
> exchanging knowledge and ideas.

The Philadelphia Connection lives today in the person of Oden Pope, musician extraordinaire. Oden met Coltrane when he was sixteen years old at the Woodbine Club and talked about his involvement with changes, methods of constructing a solo, and to phrase like Billy Eckstine and Sarah Vaughn. This year, Oden was chosen as the number one saxophone player by the people of Philadelphia People's Choice. The Transtop Resource Institute will honor Oden tonight at the Change of the Century Orchestra concert.

Even though Coltrane lived only forty years, he left behind a tremendous musical legacy, which has in many ways influenced virtually every contemporary musician and listener.

Bibliography

Cole, Bill. *John Coltrane.* New York: Schirmer Book Company. 1978.

Simpkins, Cothbert Ormond, MD. *Coltrane: A Biography.* New York:

Heredon House Publishers. 1975.

Thomas, J. C. *Chain the Trane: The Music and Mystique of John Coltrane*. Garden City, New York: Doubleday and Company. 1975.

At the time when I gave the presentation, there were only three books published about Coltrane. *John Coltrane* by Brian Priestley was published in 1987. Since 1987, there have been five books published. They are the following:

1. *Ascension: John Coltrane and His Quest* by Eric Nisenson in 1993.
2. *John Coltrane: A Discography and Musical Biography* by Yasuhiro Fujioka in 1995.
3. *Spirit Catcher: The Life and Art of John Coltrane* by John Fraim in 1996.
4. *The John Coltrane Companion* by Carl Woideck in 1998.
5. *John Coltrane: His Life and Music* by Lewis Porter in 1998.

I met Fujioka in 1995 at a book signing in New York. Jimmy Heath was also present.

Sidebar: 1/4-7/2012. I attended Jazz Educators Network Conference in Louisville, Kentucky. The conference theme was "Developing Tomorrow's Jazz Audiences Today." One of the highlights was the honoring of Dr. David N. Baker, chair of

Jacobs School of Music at Indiana University at Bloomington. He is African American. The second was a night performance by the Jason Marsalis Quartet with Jason on vibraphone and the Bass Extremes featuring Victor Wooten and Steve Bailey. Their executive skills were off the chart. I heard a young African American alto saxophonist, Brent Griffen, performing with the Phil Woods Ensemble at DePaul University. Also, Donald Meade, a jazz griot, was given the Meade Legacy Jazz Griot Award. I had spent many years listening to Donald at the International Association of Jazz Educators Conferences. Jazz musicians have many stories, but Donald had the facts, and that is what I teach to students. One of my mentors told me, "Facts are not arguable." The next conference will be in Atlanta, Georgia. I will be there.

Sidebar: 2/18/1990. On the Sunday of February 18, 1990, the Alpha Kappa Alpha Sorority, Omega Chapter; Omega Psi Phi Fraternity, Mu Omega Chapter; and Mount Olivet Tabernacle Baptist Church presented the Wynton Marsalis Septet in concert at the Mount Olivet Tabernacle Baptist Church, located at Forty-Second and Wallace Streets in Philadelphia. The septet included Wynton on trumpet, Todd Williams on soprano and tenor saxophones, Wes Anderson on alto saxophone, Wycliff Gordon on trombone, Marcus Roberts on piano, Reginald Veal on upright bass, and Herlin Riley on percussion. In the seven years I have known Wynton, he had attained world-class stature as a musician, statesman, and eloquent spokesman on the most serious issues faced by jazz listeners today: education and extinction. The next day, a workshop was given at the church. Wynton asked students who played with the Duke Ellington High School Orchestra to perform at the workshop. They were Farid Barron, who was a freshman at the New School of Music in New York; Christian McBride, who was a student at Juilliard School of Music; and John Roberts, who was a junior music magnet student at Overbrook High School. Student participants were John Kelly, a fifth grade student at Gompers Elementary School; David El-Bakara, an eighth grade student at Wilson Middle School; Jason Golley, a twelfth grade student at High School of Creative and Performing Arts; Jamel Walker, a freshman at Community College of Philadelphia; and Mike Consetino, a freshman at Temple University. Richard "Buzzy" Wilson and I promoted the concert and workshop. Buzzy died not long after this project. Richard was a baritone saxophonist and promoter.

Sidebar: 2/28/2009. Attended the funeral of Harrison Ridley Jr. (October 22, 1938-February 19, 2009) at Lutheran Church of the Holy Communion, located at 2110 Chestnut Street, Philadelphia, Pennsylvania. We all listened to his radio show *The Historical Approach to the Positive Music*, and Harrison was known for carrying shopping bags full of LPs and books. Oftentimes people would drive him home after his show on late Sunday nights. One of his many achievements was earning an honorary doctorate of music in 2005 from Villanova University. One of the courses I taught at the Community College of Philadelphia was the music of black Americans. It was an evening class, and Harrison on occasion would visit the class. One evening, I was doing a lecture on Duke Ellington and mentioned, "I do not have many examples of Ellington's orchestral music." After class, he said that he had many examples if I wanted to hear some examples. I ended up in his library, which was located in his mother's basement, and stayed all night. We would have stayed longer, but we needed to go to work. Every idea was cross-referenced. When I needed to know, I went to Harrison for the facts. I hope his collection is in a safe place so it can be made available to students. Yes, indeedy.

Ellington Project

On August 7, 1988, I met with the eastern division president of MENC. The purpose of the meeting was to explore the possibility of having the National Black Music Caucus present the Duke Ellington Orchestra at the eastern conference in Boston, Massachusetts, in 1989, made up of outstanding high school students from the eastern division. I received a letter from Dorothy A. Straub, confirming the performance and reception.

Letter from Mike Consentino—Trumpet

> Dear Mr. Allen
> I'm writing this note to thank you for all you've done to help make the Duke Ellington Orchestra such a success. Thank you for giving me the

opportunity to be a part of this terrific group. I'd
also like to thank the N.B.M.C. for sponsoring the
event. I can't wait until the concert in Philadelphia,
and hope we will have additional concerts.

Sincerely,

Michael A. Consentino

Sidebar: 1/24/2011. Attended the Schomberg Center's Eighty-
Fifth Anniversary Gala and Tribute to Howard Dodson held at
Aaron Davis Hall, the City College of New York. Howard and I
were classmates at West Chester State Teachers College. Howard
retired as director of the Schomberg Center for Research in Black
Culture, a research library of the New York Public Library and
the world's leading archive of the global black experience. The
new director is Khalil Gibran Muhammad.

On August 9, 1988, met with Dr. Warrick Carter, dean of faculty,
Berklee School of Music, to discuss the possibility of the school
hosting the orchestra in March 1989. It was a positive response.

David Berger did the arrangements for the concert.
Letter to Wynton from Dorothy Straub
Mr. Wynton Marsalis   February 24, 1989
AMG International
Edward C. Arrendell
4200 Argyle Terrace NM
Washington, D.C. 20011

Dear Mr. Marsalis:

I am so pleased that the "Re-creation of the Duke Ellington Orchestra" has become a reality. George Allen has reported that the project has been a marvelous musical and personal experience for the high school students. Unfortunately my efforts to attend last Sunday's rehearsal were unsuccessful.

I am looking forward to Friday's performance in Boston and delighted that M.E.N.C. conference participants will be able to attend this special event.

Best wishes for a fulfilling conclusion to this unique and exciting project.

Sincerely,

Dorothy A. Straub

M.E.N.C. Eastern Division President

Sidebar: 3/3/2012. Why is it that church is only on Sunday?

After attending many of Wynton's performances at jazz festivals and performance halls, the re-creation of the Duke Ellington Project started after a performance by Wynton on July 30, 1984, at the Mann Music Center, located in Fairmount Park in Philadelphia. That evening, he performed the Haydn Trumpet Concerto, Carnival of Venice, and a jazz standard, "For

All We Know." "For All We Know" was performed solo before a hushed audience. I was begging for at least one bass player to improvise a bass line, but I guess they didn't rehearse this piece. The *Philadelphia Inquirer* gave the following review:

> The music was played with what can only be called
> charm—the charm that grows from immersion in
> the music rather Than from learned stage manner.

My first intent was to ask Wynton to conduct and train an all-black jazz band of high school students from the Eastern Division of Music Educators National Conference. He said yes.

The next step was to talk to Wynton's management, AMG International and copartners Edward C. Arrendell II and Vernon Hammond. I had met Ed and Vernon in 1983 after a performance by Wynton's group at the Academy of Music. I learned then that the key to working with Wynton was to clear everything with them because Wynton says yes to many things.

On March 23, 1985, I sent them a proposal, and on June 22, 1985, they approved the project.

> Dear Vernon:
> It was good hearing from you. I do feel as you do,
> that it is time to put some things in writing. As I
> said on the telephone, I spoke with a tired Wynton
> on Monday afternoon after lunch. We did discuss
> the project but things need to be in writing.

<u>This is the project.</u>

The Eastern Region of the National Black Music Caucus [NBMC] is forming a jazz band which will be trained by Wynton. The performance will take place in Boston, MA. The first or second week in March of 1989. NBMC is an associate organization of the Music Educators National Conference [MENC] which has 75,000 members. The mission of N.B.M.C. is to perpetuate the identification, education, and performance of Black derived music; and also to identify Black performers and clinicians to be presented at local, state, and national levels.

The NBMC organization began in Atlanta, Georgia, in 1972. There was a need to establish an organization that would ensure the inclusion of black clinicians and conductors, performing groups, and the music of black American composers at national and regional conferences of MENC. It is America's largest music educator's organization. We meet at Morehouse University to protest and organize because of the lack of black participation in the conference as presenters and clinicians. The National Black Music Caucus's first national conference was held in Atlanta, Georgia, in 1989.

This is the plan.

1. Purpose To form a jazz band made up of talented Black high school students
2. Name Eastern N.B.M.C. Jazz Band
3. Where To perform at the M.E.N.C. Eastern Conference in Boston, Massachusetts March 1989
4. Why To give Black high school students an opportunity to perform at a M.E.N.C. convention with an established musician (We do not get this kind of exposure at M.E.N.C. conferences)
5. How Organize a Jazz Band Festival in May 1988 to be held in Philadelphia. The Philadelphia Chapter of N.B.M.C. will organize the festival. To have perspective students send in tapes and essays to be evaluated by Wynton by December 1988. Wynton should make the final decisions. Students will housed in Boston for three days for rehearsals.
6. Budget

PHILADELPHIA JAZZ FESTIVAL 1988

Building	$350.00
Adjudicators	300.00
Trophies	<u>100.00</u>
	$750.00

BOSTON M.E.N.C. PERFORMANCE

Telephone	$100.00
Transportation	1000.00
Housing for 24 students	600.00
Food	720.00
Awards	100.00
Music	500.00
	$3020.00

Most of the cost of the Jazz Festival will be in-kind and corporate support.

Vernon, I hope this will answer some of your questions.

Sincerely,

George E. Allen

Chairperson, Eastern Division N.B.M.C.

Project was approved June 22, 1985.

In Philadelphia, after three years of conversation about the project, on June 19, 1987, Wynton proposed that we re-create the Duke Ellington Orchestra. The lightbulb was lit. After additional planning with Wynton, on the weekend of October 7, 1988, Mark Johnson and I began auditioning students. The following letter was sent to music educators in the Eastern Division of MENC.

On August 7, 1988, I met with the eastern division president of MENC. The purpose of the meeting was to explore the possibility of having the National Black Music Caucus present the Duke Ellington Orchestra at the Eastern Division Conference in Boston, Massachusetts, in 1989. The orchestra would be made up of outstanding high school students from the eastern division. I received a letter from Dorothy A. Straub confirming the performance and reception.

On August 9, 1988, I met with Dr. Warrick Carter, dean of faculty of Berklee School of Music, to discuss the possibility of the Berklee hosting the orchestra in March 1989. It was a positive response.

Sidebar: 6/20/1988. Wynton became a father.

The following letter was sent to music educators in the eastern division.

Dear Music Educator:

The National Black Music Caucus is in the process of recreating the Duke Ellington Orchestra with high school students from the Eastern Division of M.E.N.C. In-Service Conference in Boston in March of 1989. This orchestra will be conducted by Wynton Marsalis.

Remember we are recreating the Duke Ellington Orchestra and Wynton is requiring finalists to write an essay on Duke Ellington. In order to get qualified representation from across the entire division, I need your help in identifying these students.

Please return the enclosed applications by June 1, 1988. Please note that they must be high school students in the school year 1988-89. I will set up the auditions for September, 1988.

Thank you for your cooperation in this historical event. This is a first.

Sincerely,

George E. Allen

Eastern Chairperson, N.B.M.C.

I received about twenty responses. I made calls to the music educators whom I had met through MENC and NBMC, and they responded.

Auditions were held at the following locations:

Duke Ellington High School of the Arts—Washington, DC

Wilmington School of Music—Wilmington, Delaware

New York State Building in Harlem—New York, New York

Fiorello H. LaGuardia High School—New York, New York

Arts High School—Newark, New Jersey

Philadelphia High School for Girls—Philadelphia, Pennsylvania

Mark Johnson and I selected the students based on how close their sound came to re-creating the members of the Duke Ellington Orchestra. Some positions required two students. The following students were selected.

REEDS

Johnny Hodges

William Edward Bazzelle Jr.
Senior, AI DuPont High School
Greenville, Delaware

Russell Procope

Gregory Morrison
Senior, Arts High School
Newark, New Jersey

Paul Gonsalves

Walter Blanding, Jr.
Senior, Fiorello H. LaGuardia

High School of the Arts

New York, New York

Jimmy Hamilton

Mark Thomas O'Donnell
Senior, Penn Wood High School
Lansdowne, Pennsylvania

Harry Carney

Gideon Feldstein
Sophomore, Fiorello H. LaGuardia
High School of the Arts
New York, New York

Phyllis Hill, Bass Clarinet
Senior, Weequahic High School
Newark, New Jersey

TROMBONES

Lawrence Brown

Jamal Hayes
Senior, Fiorello H. LaGuardia
High School of the Arts
New York, New York

Juan Tizol

Khadafy Khan
Junior, Fiorello H. LaGuardia High
School of the Arts
New York, New York

Britt Woodman

Jonathan Greenberg
Senior, Edward R. Morrow High
School
Brooklyn, New York

TRUMPETS

Cat Anderson

Andre Carter
Senior, Duke Ellington School of
Performing Arts
Washington, DC

Jason Golley
Junior, High School of Creative
and Performing Arts
Philadelphia, Pennsylvania

Willie Cook   Jamel Walker
                               Senior, Overbrook High School
                               Philadelphia, Pennsylvania

Clark Terry   Jafar Barron
                               Junior, Central High School
                               Philadelphia, Pennsylvania

Ray Nance   Michael A. Cosentino
                               Senior, Haverford High School
                               Haverford, Pennsylvania

                               Jeremy Sterritt, Violin
                               Senior, Fiorello H. LaGuardia
                               High School of the Arts
                               New York, New York

RHYTHM SECTION

Sam Woodyard   John Roberts
                               Sophomore, Overbrook High School
                               Philadelphia, Pennsylvania

Jimmy Blanton   Christian L. McBride
                               Senior, High School of Creative
                               and Performing Arts
                               Philadelphia, Pennsylvania

Duke Ellington   Farid Barron
                                  Senior, Central High School
                                  Philadelphia, Pennsylvania

Sidebar: 12/20/2011. Attended Overbrook High School's Annual Winter Concert, and very few Overbrook students performed. I did hear a wonderful flutist, Marie Wells. I left depressed.

Rehearsals were held in Washington, Philadelphia, and in New York. After working with Wynton's schedule, the rehearsal dates were set.

Washington

Howard University	Sunday, November 20, 1988
Howard University	Sunday, December 4, 1988
Contact Person	John Irby Howard University

Philadelphia

Temple University	Sunday, October, 30, 1988
University of the Arts	Sunday, January 28, 1989
Contact Persons	Irene McKinley Temple University
	Evan Solot University of the Arts

New York

The New School	Sunday, January 8, 1989
The New School	Sunday, February 5, 1989
The New School	Sunday, February 19, 1989
Contact Person	L. E. Howell

After the first rehearsal at Temple University, the students found out how difficult Duke Ellington's music was. The students played most of the notes but did not understand the style. It was not a good experience for the students and Wynton. In fact, Wynton had negative thoughts about the project. This was no surprise to me. Wynton decided on the repertoire. The repertoire included the "Nutcracker Suite," "Such Sweet Thunder," "KoKo," and "Sweet Thursday." I made tapes for the students. The next rehearsal went better. The tapes proved very helpful for the students.

At this point in the project, we did not have a Jimmy Hamilton or a Cat Anderson. Ronald Lamar, a former music magnet student from Overbrook High School and music educator at Penn Wood High School, recommended Mark O'Donnell for the Jimmy Hamilton chair. I found a Cat Anderson at the High School of the Creative and Performing Arts. I heard him perform with the All-City Jazz Band directed by Myer Savits, director of music education for the Philadelphia School District. Later on, Mr. Lamar assisted with the project.

Coordinating the project presented a few problems. For the December 4 rehearsal, there was a problem getting the New York group from New York to Washington because money was needed for transportation. I drove my '85 Olds Cutlass to New York to pick up the group, drove to Washington, drove back to New York, then drove back home to Philadelphia. I drove eight hundred miles that weekend. I was not asked. I went to school the next day.

On February 5, I had an accident in the Lincoln Tunnel. I was driving the Community College of Philadelphia van to transport the students from Philadelphia for the New York rehearsals. Fortunately, no one was hurt, but I totaled the van. We were a sorry sight standing in the tunnel with our instruments. Traveling by taxis, we arrived at the rehearsal on time. We returned to Philadelphia on the SEPTA Trenton Local R7. Because people were asking about the group, John Roberts and Christian McBride were self-appointed spokesmen for the group.

Attended the Jazz Education Network Conference in Louisville, Kentucky. The conference theme was "Developing Tomorrow's Jazz Audiences Today." One of the highlights was the honoring of Dr. David N. Baker, chair of the Jacobs School of Music Jazz Program at Indiana University at Bloomington, and evening performances by the Jason Marsalis Quartet and the Bass Extremes Quartet featuring Victor Wooten and Steve Bailey. Heard an outstanding young alto saxophonist who performed with the Phil Woods Ensemble from DePaul University in Chicago. Next year's conference will be in Atlanta. Donald Meade, a jazz griot, received the Meade Legacy Jazz Griot Award. I have spent many years listening to Donald at the International Association of Jazz Educator's conferences. Many musicians have stories, but Donald had the facts. Facts are not arguable.

The itinerary for this historic concert was sent to the parents and students.

Dear parents and students:

This letter will provide you with the information you will need for our historic presentation in Boston.

ITINERARY

Wednesday, March 1, 1989

Leave Philadelphia   9:00 A.M.

Overbrook High School

59th & Lancaster Ave. (215) 878-8200

ARRIVE IN NEW YORK   11:00 A.M.

LaGuardia High School

100 Amsterdam Avenue (212) 496-0700 [pick up Wynton]

ARRIVE IN BOSTON   4:30 P.M.

Mid-town Motor Inn

220 Huntingdon Ave. (617) 496-0700

DINNER   **6:00 P.M.**

Berklee School of Music

1140 Boylston Street (617) 266-1400

REHEARSAL   7:00-9:00 P.M.

Berklee School of Music

Thursday, March 2, 1989

BREAKFAST   8:00 A.M.
Berklee School of Music

REHEARSAL   9:00-11:00 A.M.
Berklee School of Music

LUNCH   11:00 A.M.

PERFORMANCE   1:00 P.M.
English High School
7th & Louis Pasteur Ave. (617) 718-6300

DINNER   5:00 P.M.
Berklee School of Music

REHEARSAL   7:00-9:00 P.M.

Friday, March 3, 1989

BREAKFAST   8:00 A.M.

PERFORMANCE   10:00 A.M.
West Rockberry High School
205 VFW Parkway (617) 323-4866

LUNCH 1:00 P.M.

Berklee School of Music

SOUND CHECK 4:00 P.M.

PERFORMANCE 6:15 P.M.

Berklee Performance Center

150 Massachusetts Ave.

Saturday, March 4, 1989

BRUNCH 11:00 A.M.

Berklee School of Music

SIGHTSEEING 12:00 to 4:00 P.M.

RECEPTION 5:30-7:00 P.M.

Marriott Hotel

Vineyard-Yarmouth Suite

ALL ORCHESTRA MEMBERS ARE TO BE PRESENT

Sunday, March 5, 1989

LEAVE BOSTON 9:00 P.M.

ARRIVE NEW YORK CITY 1:30 P.M.

LaGuardia High School

ARRIVE PHILADELPHIA 4:00 P.M.

Overbrook High School

MY ROOM ASSIGNMENTS

Room #1 Room#2 Room#3

C. McBride W. Blanding Jr. G. Morrison

J. Roberts J. Haynes Ed. Bazzelle

F. Baron G. Feldstein M. O'Donnell

J. Baron K. Khan

Room#4 Room#5 Room#6

J. Walker A. Carter P. Hill

M. Consentino J. Sterritt

J. Golley J. Greenberg

Room#7

M. Johnson

R. Lamar

THINGS TO REMEMBER

1. Tuxedo for Friday night performance
2. Suit and tie for high school performances
3. Plan ahead what you need to bring for four days

4. Be on time and at the place you should be **ALL THE TIME**. Wynton wants you to be professional and responsible young people

5. It would be helpful if you would read something about "Duke" before you arrive in Boston

6. Parents, please plan to be at the performance on Friday by 5:30 P.M. We are reserving 70 seats for the concert and 60 places for the reception.

IF YOU NEED ME, CALL ME.
GOOD LUCK AND LET'S MAKE HISTORY

Sincerely,
George E. Allen, N.B.M.C.

This is the concert program.

Sidebar: 3/18/2012. Attended birthday celebration of the Reverend Conon Thomas Wilson Stearly Logan Sr. at the African Episcopal Church of Saint Thomas. The church was founded by Absalum Jones in 1779. Father Logan was the oldest living Alpha Phi Alpha brother.

PROGRAM
DUKE ELLINGTON TRIBUTE
Wynton Marsalis, Conductor

I. NUTCRACKER SUITE

Movement Four

II. SUCH SWEET THUNDER

Such Sweet Thunder

Sonnet for Caesar

Sonnet for Hank Cing

Lady Mac

Sonnet in Search of a Moor

The Telecaster

Up and Down, Up and Down (I will Lead Them Up and

Down)

Sonnet for Sister Kate

The Star-Crossed Lovers

Madness in Great Ones

Half the Fun

Circle of Fourths

III.   KO KO

IV. SWEET THURSDAY

Transcriptions by Bill Dobbin and David Berger

With all the transportation situations, getting everyone to the rehearsals, and learning the very difficult music, it all came together at six fifteen on Friday, March 3, 1989, at the Eastern Division Conference of MENC in Boston, Massachusetts. The concert was sponsored by the NBMC and hosted by the Berklee College of Music. A second concert was held at Rutgers University—Camden on April 24, 1989, at 8:00 p.m. This concert was a fund-raiser for the TraneStop Resource Institute Inc. I was the director of education at the time for the TransStop.

In order to keep the orchestra informed about each other, I sent them updates. I called the updates, "CHECK THIS OUT." This one was dated December 28, 1989.

Dear Group:

I hope you are enjoying the holiday. I attended Wynton's Christmas concert in New York. I hope you caught it on P.B.S. Notice how Wynton has enlarged the group. He has added Wycliff Gordon from Florida A & M on trombone and Wes Anderson from Southern University on alto saxophone. Todd Williams and Wynton performed with "The Lincoln Center Classical Jazz Orchestra."

Wynton's new group will be in concert in Philadelphia on February 18th at The Mt. Olivet Church. Eric Reed from Philadelphia was on piano. There will be a youth concert the next day at the church. Farid, John, Chris, and Walter will perform. Chris and Walter performed at Temple University's club "Night Owl" in December. Jason brought an entourage. Mike, Farid, and John also made the gig. Thanks for supporting the music and your peers.

Farid did some gigs with Wynton's group this summer. John is under contract to do a recording with CBS this spring. Gregory gave his first recital at Morgan State University this fall. Edward is studying very hard at University of Delaware. Ed, are you in the jazz band?

The word is out that Mike is playing the correct changes at Temple University. He is helping Jamel with his SATs and working with a 5th grade trumpet student who Wynton asked him to help. Thanks Mike. Andre is at New Orleans University with Ellis Marsalis. I hope to see him when I attend the I.A.J.E. conference. Andre send me your school address. How is pop?

Remember seniors you should have taken the SATs and juniors the PSATs by now. By the way, some of you did not do so well the first semester. Remember you are students first, musicians second. FOR NOW.

Sincerely,

George E. Allen, N.B.M.C.

The following was taken from a school newspaper, *Common Sense*, volume VIII, number 8, April 1989, which expresses the feelings of Mark O'Donnell the day of the first rehearsal.

As we, Mark O'Donnell's Family, searched for
Presser Hall, The meeting place for our departure,
I never thought I would Feel this way on January

8, 1989. How many people get a chance to play with Wynton Marsalis? But there I was hoping I would miss the ride that would take me to the greatest musical Experience of my life. I just didn't want to go. Thoughts were Racing through my mind; not being able to play the music; looking like a fool compared to the other guys in the band; Wynton looking down at me and saying, "What the hell are you doing with that horn, son." All these anxieties increased as I saw a group of guys, instruments in hand, standing on the corner.

The ride to New York was a living hell for me. The guys in the van were talking about the gigs they'd done and who they had played with. While all this was going on, I thought I was going to die. I had never before felt so out of place. The people behind me were talking about their tour with Maynard Ferguson, and how they talked on the phone with Miles Davis. There I was, a clarinet player, with only a year of lessons, who had hardly done anything outside the walls of Penn Wood High School. For the rest of the ride, apprehension had a death-grip on my stomach.

As we arrived at the New School of Jazz, I became resigned to my fate. Unfortunately, this attitude, which had effectively fouled my stomach could not quell my fear of being incompetent.

As I walked onto the auditorium stage, I bumped into a guy wearing A leather jacket and green sweat pants. He looked familiar, then I realized this guy was Wynton Marsalis. I introduced myself and we talked for a few seconds. It hit me, he was just a regular guy.

As we rehearsed the first song, questions and doubts raced though my mind. Did I play that rhythm right? Am I in tune? Is my sound cutting through the sax section in the right way: too loud, too soft? O God, Hope he doesn't ask me to improvise.

After a grin and nod of approval from Wynton, I can't explain how good that made me feel, everything began to click. I became absorbed in the music. My worries were no longer a concern; I was having too much fun.

By the time the session was over, I was mentally, physically and emotionally drained. As I left the stage to pack up my instruments,

Wynton walked over to me and said "good job. You get a nice sound out of your horn. Listen, make sure you study those tapes and do some shedding on those solos next week." It was this compliment and various signs of approval Wynton gave me throughout the rehearsal that made the whole day worthwhile. As soon as I realized that people appreciated what I was doing, My whole outlook changed for the better.

All the graduating seniors received scholarships. We know those still in high school will follow in their footsteps. At the MENC concert, all members of the orchestra received $1,000.00 scholarships to Berklee School of Music. Mike Consentino received a full four-year competitive scholarship. This was an outstanding group of artistic and academic young people. I learned a lot from them—about "metaphysics" from Farid Barron and James Brown from Christian McBride. We all learned a lot about being noble and majestic from Wynton.

Mike Consentino wrote me this letter.

Dear Mr. Allen:

I'm writing this note to thank you for all you're done to help make the Duke Ellington Orchestra such a success. Thank you for giving me the opportunity to be a part of this terrific group. I'd also like to thank the N.B.M.C. for sponsoring the event. I can't wait until the concert in Philadelphia, and hope we have additional concerts.

Sincerely,

Michael A. Consentino

A project like this cannot be accomplished without support from parents and administrators. They worked beyond the call of duty, particularly the Philadelphia group. We used Mr. Bazzelle's van; Mrs. Barron, Mrs. Consentino, and Mrs. O'Donnell, who helped with the tuxedos; Mrs. McCullough and Mrs. Consentino, who provided the refreshments; and all the parents who helped with transportation to Temple for the first rehearsal. Mrs. Morrison made many trips on the New Jersey Turnpike, chaperoning students. Special thanks to Dr. Camille Taylor, who set up the audition space in New York and train fare when he could not drive. The parents attended the Boston concert. Also special thanks to the Berklee School of Music and Dr. Carter, dean of faculty, for his support; and administrative staff at Temple University, the New School, Howard University, and University of the Arts.

Sidebar: 2/25/2012. Attended the funeral of Mary Walker Brown. All of Mrs. Brown's three children were in the music magnet program at Overbrook High School. Donna played the flute, Flemuel III played the percussion, and Edward played the bassoon.

I was able to receive funding for this project from two major sources: the Wynton Marsalis Educational Fund and the William Penn Foundation. With Dr. Constance Clayton's help, who was the superintendent of Philadelphia public schools, we were able to cover our expenses. I did an interview for the *Inquirer* about the project. I stated, "The project needed more funding." Dr. Barnard Watson, president of the William Penn Foundation, read the article. He called Dr. Clayton and asked her, "How much money does he need?" Dr. Clayton called Overbrook and asked me how much money I needed. That afternoon, I picked up a check with the amount we needed. I was not asked.

Around 1990, I was asked to adjudicate a gospel competition at Queens College of the City College of New York. The adjudicators were Dr. Warrick Carter, Dr. Alexandria Holloway, Ms. Della Reese, Dr. Ernest Brown, and me. Dr. Stewart Gordon was the coordinator for the competition. The choirs were from the New York City region. The competition lasted two days. We were treated very well. We did this for about three years. The project was funded by the Queens College. Jimmy Heath was chair of the Jazz Studies Department at this time.

On October 23, 1993, I gave the following introductory remarks at the African American Historical and Cultural Museum, located in Philadelphia, for a two-day symposium for the Philadelphia jazz community.

Having retired from the School District of Philadelphia after thirty years, I have found my association with nonprofit organizations most challenging. In many ways, I feel like a neophyte in this very important arena, that being African American classical music. I think music education is an important piece in preserving this music. What the TraneStop brings to the table is our educational programming.

Sidebar: 3/2/2012. The fiftieth anniversary of Wilton Chamberlain's one-hundred-point game was held at the First District Plaza in Philadelphia. It was presented by the Wilton Norman Chamberlain Postal Stamp Committee. I remember one night at Haddington Recreation Center, we were standing around, getting ready to play a pickup of five-on-five. I said something to Wilt that he didn't like, and he punched me in the chest. I thought I was going to die that night. My mother always told me, "Don't let your mouth get you into trouble." Billy Cunningham and John Chaney served as cohosts.

Carter G. Woodson from his book *The Mis-Education of the Negro* (1933) states the following: "educated Negroes" have the attitude of contempt toward their own people because in their own as well as in their mixed schools, Negroes are taught to admire the Hebrew, the Greek, the Latin, and the Teuton and to despise the African. Of the hundreds of Negro high schools recently examined by the United States Bureau of Education, only eighteen offer a course taking up the history of the Negro, and in most Negro colleges and universities where the Negro is thought of, the race is studied only as a problem or dismissed as of little consequence. Woodson goes on to say that the large majority of the Negroes who have put the finishing touches in the best colleges are all but worthless in the development of their people. One of the most striking evidences of the failure of higher education among Negroes is their detachment from the masses, the very people upon whom they must eventually count for carrying out a program of progress.

How does this relate to African American classical music? Today, 1993, there is not any black university or college in African American classical music. Only white institutions grant these degrees. The African American studies program at Temple University does not have a course in music in the program. How could these students learn about our culture and not know about the music when most everything we do in our culture is couched around music? The largest jazz organization, IAJE, is not controlled by African Americans in positions of decision making. Whites control jazz education all over the world.

I do believe the system will help us support our music, but we cannot continue to operate in a 1933 mind-set. We must learn to agree on one issue. We don't agree on what to call our music. There are many white people waiting for us to take care of and control our business, and culture is part of that business.

Sidebar: 3/3/2012. Attended a memorial tribute to coach Alonzo Lewis at Chester High School. John Chaney, Sonny Hill, and Jay Norman spoke. I played with Alonzo during the '50s and '60s. He was an all-American at La Salle University in Philadelphia.

This might be a possible way to do this. In days of old, walls were used to protect the people from outside farces. Today, people can protect themselves by correct information. The concept of a system of community building is a different conceptualization of a possible present-day communication and educational network. The philosophical concept that networks these buildings is more important than the building of the network.

Mr. Reggie Workman introduced this concept to us in 1990 at the first Philadelphia International Jazz Festival/Symposium town meeting. We need to pick upon Mr. Workman's concept because he had one thirty years ago with John Coltrane.

A sequence educational program within these walls can be stronger than the physical walls and can be the correct information that can protect the community.

Thank you.

CHAPTER SIXTEEN

In 1989, I was recommended by Dr. Richard Merrell to be a board member of the Pennsylvania Music Educator Association (PMEA). We were classmates at West Chester State Teachers College. He later became chair of the Music Education Department at the college. When I joined the board, I was the only African American. Later, Ron Booker from the Pittsburg region became a member. I was a board member from 1989 to 1999. PMEA is a statewide nonprofit organization of over five thousand members dedicated to promoting the musical development of all Pennsylvanians.

The mission of PMEA is to advance music education by encouraging excellence in the study and making of music. PMEA's vision is to continue to be the most authoritative, influential voice of music as an essential part of education throughout the Commonwealth of Pennsylvania.

The present membership evolved from a small group of band directors dating from 1933. Today, the organization includes those engaged in music instruction at all levels, from preschool to college and university, as well as those in the music industry, merchandising, and publishing. The organization promotes and supports quality music education, learning, and performance as well as promoting and supporting music education in schools and communities. PMEA is affiliated with the National Association for Music Education (NAfME), which has sixty-five thousand members. In 2012, MENC changed the name to NAfME.

Sidebar: 3/18/2012. Attended the Academy of Vocal Arts "Jubilate" concert conducted by David Antony Lofton, one of Philadelphia's underrated conductors. I played under him for the Opera on the Square concerts during "Welcome America" celebrations.

PMEA started out as the Pennsylvania Bandmasters Association in 1933 and in the following year sponsored the first All-State High School Band Festival. In 1935, the organization became the Pennsylvania School Band and Orchestra Association. With the inclusion of high school choral directors, there was another name change, the Pennsylvania School Music Association. In 1980, PSMA became affiliated with MENC. In 1947, to keep Pennsylvania with the MENC state affiliates, the association name was changed for the final time, the Pennsylvania Music Educators Association.

I became a member of PMEA in 1957 as a music education major at West Chester Teachers College. I have been a member for fifty-five years. As a high school student, I participated in district, regional, and state festivals as a clarinetist. I believe my participation in PMEA festivals helped me to be accepted into the music education program at West Chester. Mr. Carson, who auditioned me, was a member of PMEA and had heard me perform at the festivals. In 1954, I was the principal clarinetist in the All-State Band. I was not asked to audition for the All-State Orchestra.

Every year, there is an in-service conference held at different locations throughout the state. This year, 2012, it was held in Lancaster, Pennsylvania. I was the only one from Philadelphia. I only saw four African American music educators. There were only a few African Americans in the All-State performing groups, which include about six hundred students.

As a member of the PMEA board, one of my goals was to increase the participation of African Americans in PMEA. Trips were made to Pittsburg and Harrisburg at my own expense to encourage African Americans to participate. I have not been successful not only for PMEA but also for MEfME. One of the reasons given is that the literature does not have many brown faces as clinicians. One would think that there were very few African American Music Educators doing outstanding teaching. The ones that I see at conferences are the same faces. I know most of them locally and nationally. This was one of the reasons the NBMC was formed in Atlanta in 1972.

Having had the opportunity to participate in PMEA as a high school student, I realized that music was not only happening in Philadelphia. I learned that there were some very talented students in the state. If I had not had this experience, I would have had a narrow view of music in Pennsylvania.

Sidebar: 4/2/2012. Heard a live performance of the Carl Nielsen Clarinet Concerto performed by Benito Meza, a product of the El Sistema program in Venezuela. It brought back memories when I played it with the Symphony Club. Arthur Cohn was the conductor.

My main purpose in attending conferences was to keep informed of the latest methods and materials so I could adapt them for my students. My students didn't have many of the materials many schools had, even in Philadelphia. I really wanted to know what the better-funded school districts were doing in music education. This proved to be helpful, me becoming a better music educator. It is not good that too many African American music educators do not have many questions as they relate to music education. Many have become reactive than proactive. When my administrators would ask me, "How did you do that?" I would say, "I don't know, just did it." But I did know. The sad thing about all this is African American music educators do not attend professional conferences. Those who do attend have been attending for years. I don't see young people at these conferences, and if I do, most of them are undergrad students attending because it is part of their curriculum.

In April 1990, I presented at the PMEA In-Service Conference the following paper, "The Realities of the Changing Demographics of America's Music Classroom."

In the twenty-first century, ethnic groups in the United States will outnumber whites for the first time. The "browning of America" will alter everything in society, from politics and education to industry, values, and culture.

Today, one American in four defines himself or herself as Hispanic or nonwhite. The typical US citizen who traces his or her descent in a direct line to Europe will be part of the past by the twenty-first century. By the time elementary students in classrooms today reach midlife, their diverse ethnic experiences in the classroom will be generalized in their neighborhoods and workplaces throughout the United States. The Census Bureau reported that over the last decade, the number of Asian Americans has more than doubled and the Hispanic population has grown by more than 50 percent, underscoring the extraordinary pace of change in the nation's racial and ethnic profile. Cultural diversity probably accelerated more in the 1990s than any other decade, according to Carl Haub, a demographer for the Population Reference Bureau, a research group. While large portions of the Asian and Hispanic population still live in California and a handful of other states, the 1980s saw a wave of movement among these groups into virtually every state, community, and music classroom. In Minnesota, for example, the number of Asians rose from 26,536 in 1980 to 77,886 in 1990.

Sidebar: 4/11/2012. Went to Peter Nero and the Philly Pops concert to hear Joseph Smith perform the Arti Shaw Clarinet Concerto. Joe studied with my clarinet teacher. Concert was at the Kimmel Center for the Performing Arts in Philadelphia, Pennsylvania.

According to recently released numbers in 1990 via a Philadelphia-area-wide census, the nonwhite population grew to 402,715—to 12 percent from 10 percent in 1990. Many of the communities surrounding Philadelphia have more black and Asian faces today than they had a decade ago. Douglas S. Massey, professor of sociology and public studies at the University of Chicago, states that all-white communities are becoming quite rare in metropolitan areas around the country. In 1990, the eight-county Philadelphia metropolitan area was home to a higher percentage of racial minorities than the nation as a whole. Last year, 23 percent of the region's residents were nonwhite, compared with 20 percent across the nation.

In the March 23, 1991, edition of the *Philadelphia Inquirer,* an article by Murry Bubin and Meill A. Borowski entitled "Philadelphia Suburbs Edging toward More Diversity" makes the following observations:

1. Growing numbers of black residents have moved from the city to the suburbs. The white population has shown little growth.
2. Yeadon's black population grew from about one-third of the total in 1980 to two-thirds in 1990. In 1970, only 15 percent of the population was black.
3. Lower Bucks County's phone book has 138 listings for Patels. Patel is the Asian Indian equivalent of our Smith or Jones.

4. The community of Willingboro in Burlington County, New Jersey, formerly Levittown, was 40 percent white and 50 percent black in 1990, almost the mirror image of the 1980 figures, 59 percent white and 30 percent black.

5. In 1980, 98 percent of Cheltenham's population was white. Today, 79 percent are white, 15 percent are black, and 5 percent are Asian.

6. In Chester County, the number of Hispanics jumped to 49 percent. However, many are mushroom pickers and farmworkers with incomes that make home ownership in this county nothing but a dream.

7. In the seven-block-by-one-block Delaware County borough of Millbourne, the Asian population grew elevenfold in the decade from 34 to 374, 45 percent of the town's residents.

The change in the suburban populations has brought other changes, large and small. These changes will be discussed later when I discuss their impact on education.

If current trends in immigration and birthrates persist, the Hispanic population will have further increased to an estimated 21 percent, the Asian presence about 22 percent, blacks almost 12 percent, and whites a little more than 2 percent when the twentieth century ends. According to William A. Henry III, the number of US residents who are Hispanic or nonwhite will have more than doubled to nearly 115 million while the white population will not increase at all. By 2056, when a person born in 1990 will be 66 years old, the "average" US resident, as defined by census statistics, will trace his or her descent to Africa, Asia, the Hispanic world, the Pacific Islands, Arabia: almost anywhere but white Europe. "Once America was a microcosm of European nationalities," says Dr. Molefi Asante, chairman of the first university to offer a doctoral in African American studies, Temple University. He continues by stating that "today America is a microcosm of the world."

The statistical demographics impinge on our music classrooms today and will continue into the twenty-first century. In New York State, about 40 percent of the elementary and secondary school children belong to an ethnic minority, and in California, white students are already a minority. Because Hispanics are so numerous and Asians such a fast-growing group, they have become the "hot minorities." Blacks are no longer the "hot minority."

The projected Philadelphia School District population indicates that enrollment will increase over the five years (90-95) by 13,489 or 6.5 percent. The interesting demographic is that the black population will decrease and the Hispanic and Asian population will increase. The white population will drop 1.5 percent.

There are social realities that result from these changing demographics. The following are a few issues we need to know as music educators. One, as music educators, we are the key because all our students bring their music with them every day. Two, we should acquaint ourselves with some of the songs/stories they bring particularly from the urban setting. This is from Alex Kotiowitz's book *There Are No Children Here* (Doubleday 1991). "Lefie, age twelve, is changing quickly from sweet to sulky. He has become so angry about his drug-induced father, the firebombing he witnessed out his window, the murder he has seen and a federal agent's killing of a young friend." Three, the *New York Times* series Children of the Shadows, April 4, 1993, shows a fourth-grade student acting as an adult for his little sister. In a book-review section of the *Philadelphia Inquirer,* H. G. Bissinger reviews Nicholas Lemann's book, *The Promised Land,* and states the following: "The only difference between a sharecropper's shack in the south and the housing project in the north was that one was bigger than the other."

America's oldest and most vibrant Puerto Rican community is just north of Harlem where the per capita income is $4,000/year. One out of seven adults is out of work. More than one in three gets some form of public assistance, among the highest welfare rates in the nation. The area has some of the city's worst crime and some of the nation's highest school-dropout rates. Drugs and AIDS haunt every man, woman, and child who live in east Harlem. A woman's work is never done in el barrio (Spanish Harlem), where nearly half of all households (48 percent) are headed by females, one of the highest ratios in the United States.

Sidebar: 4/26/2012. Heard a performance of Brahms's Symphony no. 3 in F Major with the Philadelphia Orchestra. I mentioned to one of my former music teachers that I heard some new interpretations. The response was "It was just new balancing." I was listening to the music. Simon Rattles was the conductor.

The changing demographics in the rural communities result in different kinds of social realities. In an article by William A. Henry in *Time Magazine*, "Beyond the Melting Pot," states the following: "At the Sesame Hut Restaurant in Houston, a Korean immigrant owner trains Hispanic immigrant workers to prepare Chinese-style food for a largely Black clientele." In California, whites of all ages account for just 58 percent of the population, and in San Jose, bearers of the Vietnamese surname Nguyen (New An) outnumber the Jones in the telephone directory fourteen columns to eight. Dr. Bill Brantley, director of Administration Operations and Pupil Services for the West Chester Area School District, stated that blacks and other minorities represent 42 percent of the population who reside outside of the boundaries of the West Chester Area School District, and 58 percent live within the school district of seventy square miles. Dr. Brantley also said that the Hispanics are getting more in the mainstream and therefore are not migrating from the area.

With this kind of social and demographic reality, do we need to start to do things differently in the music classroom? I think so, and particularly in music. In the *Harvard Educational Review*, Lisa D. Delpit eloquently describes a personal reality.

"Why do the refrains of progressive education movements seem lacking in the diverse harmonies, the variegated rhythms, and the shades of tone expected in a truly heterogeneous chorus? Why do we hear so little representation from the multicultural voices which comprise the present-day American educational scene?" In the "Browning of America," many minorities are still asking the same questions.

If students are to learn a multicultural perspective, music teachers need to develop an educational philosophy that recognizes the inherent worth of endeavors by different cultural groups. A multicultural approach to music learning in American schools is important for two reasons. One, people from more than one hundred world cultures now reside in the United States, and some ethnic groups now number in the tens of thousands or millions that come from Asia, and another 40 percent are from Mexico, Central and South America, and the Caribbean. Two, the concept of America being a melting pot is clearly waning. Thus, today the United States is best described as a country composed of a mosaic of various ethnic communities that contribute to the national culture as they maintain distinct identities. A superintendent of the Milwaukee public schools remarked that in a visit to one of his schools, the pupils displayed a sign that said "Welcome" in twenty-seven different languages because these languages were represented at that one school. Do you know what ethnic cultures are in your school? On a visit to a school west of Philadelphia, I asked the music teacher, "How many Blacks are in the school?" He said, "I don't know."

A multicultural approach to music education is clearly in keeping with perhaps the most important trend of the past forty years, and there is the growing understanding of music as a world phenomenon. In many of the major records stores, there is a world music section. The research of many distinguished ethnomusicologists has shown that the world contains a number of highly sophisticated musical traditions that are based on different but equally logical principles. One must learn the operative principles of any tradition in order to understand it.

Sidebar: 5/29/2012. Donald Wilson passed on May 17, 2012. I remember Don playing in the Tony Williams Quartet at LaRose Jazz Club on Monday nights. He was the perfect accompanist. He could play in any style and tonality, expressly on open mike. He will be missed.

In the past, as a result of emphasizing selected aspects of western European and American classical and folk music, American teachers have often (and too often) led students to believe that there was only one major system in the world, the Euro-American system. Today's scholars have clearly demonstrated that educational institutions at all levels need to ensure that music curricula contain balanced programs that are representative of the world and also of the multicultural nature of the United States itself.

The MENC has given paramount attention to the multicultural aspect of music education. Numerous sessions on various musical traditions have been presented at national, regional, and state conventions. Furthermore, a number of the national and international organizations, including the Society for Ethnomusicology and the International Society for Music Education, have strongly endorsed the study of world musics at all levels of instruction. To support the increased interest in a multicultural approach to music education, many books, recordings, and film companies are producing materials on world musics.

Multicultural music study can provide a number of musical outcomes for students.

1. Students are introduced to a great variety of musical sounds from all over the world.
2. Students are beginning to realize that many equally sophisticated music cultures are found throughout the globe and that Western classical music is one of many styles.
3. Students discover that musics from other cultures often have principles that differ significantly from those principles contained in music of their own culture and that one should learn the distinction and the inherent logic of each type.
4. Students increase their ability to perform, listen intelligently, and audiate many styles of music.

With this kind of objectivity, students are much less prone to judge a new music without first trying to understand it.

Are our music-teacher-training institutions preparing their students to meet this challenge of the "browning of America"?

I think we can do a better job. Today, the most appropriate training in music education should be one that will nurture the capacities and provide skills to comprehend a multiracial, multiethnic orientation. This would help to promote respect for a wide range of cultural groups. If projections prove accurate, we will become a nation increasingly isolated from western European traditions and more influenced and affected by those of African, Asian, and Hispanic origin.

Sidebar: 6/1/2012. Diane Monroe, violinist, performed in a concert of two premieres at the Curtis Institute of Music. She performed "Sonata for Violin and Piano" by Robert Capanna. Capanna is the former director of Settlement Music School. The second premiere was Sonata no. 2 for Violin and Piano by Philip Maneval, the executive director of the Philadelphia Chamber Music Society. Diane is one of my heroes. If it has a musical sound, she can perform it.

The college-music-teaching community must consider these and other signs of our times for the responsibility they have on the future work of the professional music educator. A personal observation of mine is that much of the current population in America does not spiritually identify with art music of the western European tradition. It seems the better part of wisdom to view this shift as an opportunity to expand our educational base in order to reflect the cultural resources in our society. In many cases, the "right music" has been taught to the group that maintains the institution. Students and teachers have been recruited, selected, and socialized to maintain a particular European mind-set. In a changing society, institutions must reconsider the forces underlying these practices and the message they convey to the larger community.

Sidebar: 6/12-23/2012. Attended the DuPont Clifford Brown Jazz Festival. I heard a sixteen-year-old trombonist in the Christian McBride Big Band. He reminded me of the first time I heard Lee Morgan with the Dizzy Gillespie Big Band at Pep's Musical Bar in Philadelphia. I was impressed with the pianist with a group called Hiromi. What a fine musician. I hope she is teaching somewhere. The festival is an excellent venue.

There is mounting evidence that monocultural education to the degree that students are required to deny their heritage and to adopt a new one has a deleterious effect on individuals, students, family groups, and societies. To quote the College Music Society Report: "Art music is virtually absent from the daily lives of most young people, and popular music culture is virtually absent from academia." I hope that music educators will begin to believe the mosaic.

In closing, I will read a poem from "Poetry for People" by Carol Cornwell.

The Learning Gate

Do you like what you see
Every time you look at me?
My full lips

In 1990, I submitted a paper to the curriculum/instruction chair of PMEA, "Recruitment and Retention of African Americans in Pennsylvania Music Educators Association Performing Groups: 'In Case You Missed It.'" The following are excerpts from my paper.

Recruitment and retention of African American students in music programs have become an issue that must be addressed by music educators, administrators, and the community. The number of African Americans enrolled in music programs is declining to the point that the entire music profession is facing a loss of the potential productivity and musicianship of many African American students.

Dr. Robert Atwell, president of the American Council on Education, states, "The single most important issue we face . . . is minority participation at all levels . . . we've got to turn this problem around." At the PMEA board meeting in August 1989, they recognized this problem.

Sidebar: 7/20/2012. Attended the funeral of Adrienne Carol Wescott last Friday at Zion Baptist Church in Ambler, Pennsylvania. She and her husband, Harry, were music magnet students at Overbrook High School. Adrienne passed on Friday, July 13, 2012. She was one of the faithful members of the Overbrook Singers. They sang at the funeral. It was good seeing former students.

It is unfair to place the burden of responsibility of a lack of African American students in performing groups on the public schools alone. Surely, our entire society has to assume some responsibility for not insisting that the African American students become a part of America's musical heritage. Our society in general possesses the stereotypical belief that African Americans respond only to certain genres of music. Charles Hoffer, past president of MENC, expressed this view.

> There is the repertoire that most of the outstanding (predominantly white) performing groups perform. Usually students generally do not relate to it very much. Minority students generally do not relate to it very much. They come from a different heritage and they justifiably take pride in their musical traditions. They feel more comfortable, as well as more competent, when performing the music that is familiar to them.

This is an attitude that I have observed in too many music educators. African American students who are subjected to professional musicians and educators bearing similar attitudes are subtly told that they should not expect to be able to perform the "general repertoire." Is it any wonder that minority participation in music-performing groups has declined? I remember my son George not given the opportunity to perform with the top-performing groups at Temple University. I transferred him to West Chester University, where he was allowed to perform the "general repertoire." I also remember my clarinet teacher telling me, "Don't let anyone tell you, you can't play." I was also told I could not teach.

James J. Dunderstadt, president of the University of Michigan, states that

> perhaps no arena in American culture has been so visibly enriched by African American contributions as the performing arts . . . Indeed, the artistic culture of America would be a different product—an immeasurably poorer one—without the contributions of African American musicians and composers.

I believe that music programs in Pennsylvania are immeasurably poorer when I attend all-state performances and I see only five African Americans performing. Together, we can turn this situation around, in case you missed it.

Sidebar: 7/25/2012. I attended two wonderful concerts this week: the Big Sing//Schubert and the Chester Children's Chorus. Three choirs participated in the Big Sing//Schubert. They were the Mendelssohn Club of Philadelphia, conductor Alan Harler; the African Episcopal Church of Saint Thomas, conductor Dr. Jay Fluellen; and the Philadelphia Master Chorale, conductor Changho Lee. Each choir performed a selection composed by Schubert and combined choirs for a performance of Franz Schubert's "Mass in G."

The second concert was by the Chester Children's Chorus at Lang Concert Hall at Swarthmore College. There are 140 students in the four choirs, which performed individually and combined for a performance of the Mozart requiem. Dr. John Alston is the director of the chorus and is an associate professor of music at Swarthmore College. They are from Chester, Pennsylvania.

Unfortunately, the socioeconomic conditions of many African Americans have not allowed them the opportunities or luxury of pursuing music as a career. In addition, many African American parents do not fully realize the long-term commitment in the performing arts. It takes about twenty years to deliver a student to the audition. This inability on the part of some parents and students to realistically access what has to be done in order to prepare for a career in music and then to do it has clearly contributed to the high attrition rate of African Americans in school music programs. I told my parents that the arts are a part of being educated. Many were not aware of this.

Special attention needs to be given to the area of African American males. Young African American males represent a special problem in schools. Here are some of the factors that place them at a special disadvantage.

1. Their teachers appear to them as alien, hostile, and even menacing, including middle-class African American teachers. If this is so and the teacher expects less, it should not surprise us that African American male students achieve less.

2. African American males do less than their female counterparts in the job market. They see less utility in classroom performance.

3. The male role model is frequently absent. They are more likely than any other group to grow up in families that do not include a parent of their own gender. "African American females usually have their mothers to teach them how responsible women are expected to behave," according to William Raspberry in the August 29, 1990, issue of *The Inquirer*.

African American males may be peculiarly susceptible to learning the lessons of manhood not from their homes but from the streets. They take care of themselves in physical rather than intellectual ways, and this is the reason that so many of them scorn academics as either effeminate or something that "white folks do."

It must be said that much legislation designed to reduce social inequality was passed during the sixties; however, only a few African Americans were notably influenced by increased opportunities in employment, housing, and education. What we saw instead was most African Americans remained below the national income average, continued to live in blighted physical environments, and attended segregated, inferior schools. How did I know these things in 1982?

In the February 1982 issue of *Harvard Education Review*, it states the following from a *Newsweek* article:

> The middle-class fourth of the black population often written about as "burgeoning" has in fact, not grown in a decade. And the fourth living in poverty has not shrunk. But the rate of black unemployment has doubled since 1969, to 11.5% . . . and the number of unemployed blacks has nearly tripled to 1.4 million. The rates run devastatingly high among black teenagers; a new generation is coming of riot age with short work, few skills, stunted hopes—and no memory whatever of the victories so painfully won by their parents.

What can we do as music educators about this situation in order to bring about recruitment and retention of African American students in PMEA performing groups? In case you missed it.

I think all of us must accept the fact that Pennsylvania has a problem in this area. Dr. Rene Boyer-White, a past president of NBMC, states the following solutions. First, there has to be a collaborative effort of music, performance, and education at the university level and music specialists in our public schools. Second, there must be a serious attempt to adapt curricula and programs in our school to fit the needs of our ever-increasing ethnic population in this country. Dr. Boyer-White goes on to say in the December 1989 issue of *Music Educators Journal*:

> The future of education will depend on teachers who can think beyond cultural boundaries. Knowledge pertaining to different cultural practices will become increasingly necessary to successful functioning in an interdependent world.

With this in mind, how can we begin?

1. We must rethink who the students are—the ones we are educating.
2. Duality music programs must be from kindergarten to twelfth grade.
3. Administrators, counselors, teachers, and parents of African American students must be awakened to the fact that a student's training must begin at an early age.
4. A quality broad-based African American instruction should be provided by a certified and qualified music educator on all levels, not just the general music teacher.
5. African American student development should be assessed and reported to the parent(s) on a regular basis. One way

to do this is to administer the musical aptitude profile developed by Dr. Edwin Gordon at Temple University.

6. Handbooks should be handed to parents who seek information about programs or individuals who will enhance African American student development beyond the classroom. Seek the support of African American musicians in the community.

7. Financial aid programs to assist needy but qualified African American students in financing private lessons at the junior high and high school levels should be established.

8. Networking with predominantly black colleges and universities is important because they are role models for African American students.

Some of you might have a problem with this, but have no fear. We have many fine music programs besides Florida A & M, Howard University, and Morgan State University. These institutions help African American students with establishing their identities and learning who they are. At the NBMC conference in Atlanta, the level of performance would equal an MENC or PMEA conference.

The National Association of School Musicians reported that black faculty constituted 3.6 percent of the total faculty members in reporting NASM schools, and 65.2 percent had no black faculty. If there are few or, in some situations, no minority faculty members or graduate students, how or why should African American students aspire to such a role?

"Teacher-training institutions must make concentrated efforts to prepare qualified music educators who understand and can overcome the current cultural and sociological attitudes about minority participation in the arts," according to Boyer-White (1989). Teacher-training institutions must have materials for teachers to learn about black music. This was difficult in the past because the music of black composers was not included in major music encyclopedias until 1978. The following are suggested resource materials that should be accessible to all music educators.

1. *A Concordance of Scores and Recordings of Music of Black Composers* by Dr. Dominque Rene' deLerma (1984). *Black Music Research Journal,* Columbia College, Chicago, Illinois 60605.

2. CBS Records Black Composers series contains nine recordings and a sixteen-page booklet. The Black Composers series contains music written by black composers during the eighteenth, nineteenth, and twentieth centuries out of the black aesthetic in the western concert music tradition over a two-hundred-year period (the College Music Society, 1444 Fiftieth Street, Boulder, Colorado 80302).

3. *Biographical Dictionary of Afro-American and African Musicians* (1982) by Eileen Southern. There are 418 pages

with three appendices: period of birth, place of birth, and musician occupations (Greenwood Press, Westport, Connecticut).

4. *The New Grove Dictionary of Jazz* (1982) edited by Barry Kernfeld, two volumes. (Macmillan Press Limited, London).

5. *The Music of Black Americans: A History* (1971) by Eileen Southern. Includes a bibliography and discography (W. W. Norton & Co. Inc., New York).

6. *Multicultural Perspectives in Music Education* (1989) MENC. Gives examples of teaching strategies from a multicultural perspective.

I would like for the reader to be aware of what PMEA has done to address this important situation. On February 12, 1990, at West Chester University, an action plan was established by Richard Merrell, J. Hotz, and me. The most important part of the action plan was to move slowly and to think small. To this end, we are only working two districts, 10 and 12. We will add the remaining ten districts later. District 12 has identified five high schools that will prepare and send African American students to district auditions. They are four schools from Philadelphia and one from Chester.

On June 4, 1990, I met with District 10 teachers from Bethlehem, Easton, and Allentown at Freedom High School. Let me share some information that resulted from this meeting. In the Allentown/Bethlehem/Eastern areas, there are no African

American music educators and the average African American high school population is 6 percent. The group felt that they were doing an adequate job encouraging participation in PMEA's performing groups, based on percentages of African Americans in their schools. In their opinion, a realistic goal for the district would be to maintain the same percentages in district, regional, and state performing groups. There are sixty-one high schools in District 10.

The following are statistics from the Pennsylvania Department of Education for the school year 1989-1990 of African American students in four school districts in District 10 from K-12.

	African Americans	Total	% of African Americans
1. Reading	1,682	11,899	14%
2. Allentown	1,227	13,396	9%
3. Bethlehem	526	11,907	4%
4. Easton	651	6,542	9%

District 10's average African American school population is 10 percent. How is the district able to produce championship basketball, track, and football teams with only 10 percent African Americans?

What I have been talking about is a personal attitude toward African American students in our schools today—not in the past. Today's students bring many concepts and feelings into your classrooms and rehearsals. Notice, I'm talking about students who are in your classrooms and rehearsals, not the students who choose not to attend. Let them know they have made an important contribution to America's music. Everybody has two heritages: their ethnic heritage and human heritage. "The human aspects give art its real enduring power, not the racial aspects (Stanley Crouch, *DownBeat*, September 1990).

We are proud of our marvelous heritage of spirituals, work songs, blues, gospel, ragtime, jazz, pop, and rhythm and blues. We excel as performers, conductors, educators, composers, and entrepreneurs. Therefore, I am very proud and most anxious to share this and hopefully make this wonderful music accessible to all students in Pennsylvania.

May I make two suggestions that have helped me to share this music with students. One, I changed my attitude about the prioritizing of music. Duke Ellington said there are only two kinds of music: good and bad. Two, make sounds in your classrooms. General music teachers, stop lecturing; vocal teachers, come from behind the podium; and theory and music history teachers, stop giving all the facts. Music is sound. Let the students make music.

You know it is a good education for all students to understand and appreciate African American music. We all need to make changes in our attitudes.

The demographics have changed. In 2010, Eugene Robinson, Pulitzer Prize winner, states the following in his book, *Disintegration: The Splintering of Black America.*

The African American population in the United States has always been seen as a single entity: a black America with unified interest and needs. Eugene Robinson argues that over decades of desegregation, affirmative action and immigration the concept of a black America, now there are four:

- A Mainstream middle-class majority with a full ownership stake in American society;
- A large Abandoned minority with less hope of escaping poverty and dysfunction than at anytime since Reconstructions crushing end;
- a small Transcendent elite with such enormous wealth, power and influence that even white folks have to genuflect;
- and two newly Emergent groups-individuals of mixed-race heritage and communities of recent black immigrants that make us wonder what 'black' is even supposed to mean.

Robinson continues, "What's more, these groups have become so distinct that they view each other with mistrust and apprehension." Robinson's book is published by Doubleday.

I received the June 2012 issue of *Music Educators Journal*, and it included the following articles.

1. "Social Class and School Music" by Vincent C. Bates
2. "Missing Faces from the Orchestra: An Issue of Social Justice?" by Lisa C. DeLorenzo
3. "Social Justice and Music Education: The Call for a Public Pedagogy" by Randall Everett Allsup and Eric Shieh
4. "Cultural Diversity and the Formation of Identity: Our Role as Music Teachers" by Kate R. Fitzpatrick
5. "Performing Our World: Affirming Cultural Diversity through Music Education" by Adria R. Hoffman
6. "Music Education behind Bars: Giving Voice to the Inmates and the Students Who Teach Them" by Frank Abrahams, Miranda M. Rowland, and Kristian C. Kohler
7. "The Skin that We Sing: Culturally Responsive Choral Music Education" by Julia Shaw

This is in volume 98, number 4, June 2012 of *Music Educators Journal*. This should be required reading in all music methods classes. I wonder if beginning African American music educators have an opportunity to read these articles. I thought I knew everything about African Americans when I was a beginning music educator. I did not begin to learn until I attended MENC in Atlanta in 1972 and saw over two hundred African American music educators at Morehouse University and attending the Symposium on Black American Music held on the Ann Arbor campus of the University of Michigan, August 9-15, 1985.

Sidebar: 8/14/2012. Received a call from Brian Evans stating "Harry Paul Dixon passed on today in Japan." He was one of my music students at Gratz Senior High School. After graduating, he played with many groups, including Force of Nature and Soul Devalents. Harry was a great trumpeter and musician. The funeral was held at the Most Precious Blood Catholic Church at Twenty-Eighth and Diamond Street, Philadelphia, Pennsylvania 19121, on Thursday, August 30, 2012.

The second impact was me attending the Black American Music Symposium held in Ann Arbor, Michigan. The symposium was the first of its kind and was organized by Willis C. Patterson, full professor in voice at the university. The symposium involved many of the most important scholars and performers of black music in America, including Undine Moore, Hale Smith, Kermit Moore, Billy Taylor, Eva Jessye, Eileen Southern, among many others. I didn't know that this level of scholarship and musicianship existed among African Americans. I only knew what was going on in Philadelphia. Philadelphia had only three African Americans in the Philadelphia Orchestra and a few outstanding musicians I would see in some of the performing groups. We had very few teaching at the academy. In 1985, Temple might have had one, and West Chester did not have any full-time professors. I had been told by a Philadelphia music supervisor that music schools in the south could only play marches. I thought I knew, but after Atlanta and Ann Arbor, I know we can do it all. That might be the problem. I left Ann Arbor with the feeling that black folks are in charge of music in heaven.

Sidebar: 10/6/2012. I attended two funerals, Alice Dolores Hamilton and Ronald Harrison Ford. Dolores passed on September 28, 2012. We graduated from Overbrook High School in 1954. She was the treasurer, secretary, and webmaster for the Overbrook High School Alumni Association. She was an exceptional athlete and played for Philadelphia's first professional women's basketball team, the Rockettes. Ron passed on September 29, 2012. Ron was a graduate of Cheyney University and was one of the best guards to play basketball at the university. His best friend was Ed Williams, an administrator for the Philadelphia School District. We played basketball together at the Sherwood Recreation Center at Fifty-Sixth and Christian Street in West Philadelphia. Ron retired from Overbrook as a teacher, mentor, and basketball coach.

I took my family and some of my wife's family to the symposium. I also invited relatives who lived in Detroit. They wanted more. They didn't know either. The following are some of the symposium topics and performances.

Teaching Black American Music: Part I, "Teacher Education in Music for 1990s: Input from the Black Perspective"

Reginald Buckner (moderator), professor of music (jazz studies) and Afro-American studies, School of Music and College of

Liberal Arts, University of Minnesota. *Alvin Batiste*, professor
of music (clarinet and jazz), Southern University, Baton Rouge,
Louisiana. *Eddie Meadows*, professor of music (music education),
San Diego State University. *William Theodore McDaniel Jr.*,
professor of jazz and Afro-American music.

Carlesta Henderson, professor of music (music education),
Division of Arts and Humanities, Keene State College, Keene,
New Hampshire; president, National Black Music Caucus
(MENC).

"Musique d'Afrique Nouvelle Orleans" composed and
performed by clarinetist Alvin Batiste.

"Suite for Orchestra and Jazz Piano" composed and
performed by Billy Taylor.

Black Music Research

Samuel Floyd (moderator), professor of music and director of
Center for Black Music Research, Columbia College, Chicago,
Illinois. *Dominique Rene de Lerma*, professor of music and
graduate music coordinator, Morgan State University, Baltimore,
Maryland. *Geneva Southall*, professor of Afro-American music,
University of Minnesota. *Richard Crawford*, professor of music
history, University of Michigan, Ann Arbor, Michigan.

Performing Black American Music: Early Pioneers

Hansonia Caldwell (moderator), dean, College of Arts,
University of California at Dominquez Hills. *Eva Jessye*,
composer, conductor, author, ambassador of the arts. *Jester*

Hairston, composer, conductor, Los Angeles, California. *Undine Smith Moore*, composer.

Performance and Non-Performance of Black American Music

Hale Smith (moderator), composer, professor of music, University of Connecticut at Shorrs. *Frederick Tillis*, director, Fine Arts Center, University of Massachusetts. *Kermit Moore*, cellist, composer, conductor, New York City. *Ulysses Kay*, composer and distinguished professor of music, Lehman College, New York. *T. J. Anderson*, composer and distinguished professor of music, Tufts University, Massachuetts.

Sidebar: 10/24/2012. I attended two concerts at Temple's Boyer College of Music and Dance at the Temple Performing Arts Center. The first was a choral concert by the University Singers, with Mitos Andaya (conductor); University Women's Chorus, with John Sall (conductor); and University Chorale, with Dr. Rollo Dilworth (conductor). Dr. Dilworth was appointed chair of the Music Education Department. He is the first African American to chair a department in the school of music. There were about seven African Americans in the three choirs. The second concert was the university orchestra on October 25. They performed the Piano Concerto, Op. 38, by Samuel Barber with Clipper Erickson as soloist and "Pavane pour une infant defunte" and Daphnis et Chloe, Suite no. 2 by Maurice Ravel. There was an excellent flute solo by Justin Holguin, an African American. There were six African Americans in the orchestra.

Black American Music: Jazz Part II (History)

Warrick Carter (moderator), dean of the faculty, Berklee School of Music. *Alvin Batiste*, professor of music and director of jazz program, Southern University, Baton Rouge, Louisiana. *Bob James*, jazz pianist, recording artist, New York. *Frank Tirro*, dean, School of Music, Yale University. *Reginald Buckner*, jazz pianist, professor of music, University of Minnesota.

Chamber Music Concert

Sport for Strings	Adolphus Hailstork
Symphonietta	Coleridge-Taylor Perkinson
Lyric for Strings	George Walker
Alous	Ulysses Kay

Performing Black American Music: Recent Pioneers

George Shirley (moderator), professor of music, University of Maryland, formerly with Metropolitan Opera. *Robert McFerrin*, formerly with the Metropolitan Opera. *William Foster*, director of bands and chairman of Music Department, Florida A & M University. *Betty Allen*, director, Harlem School of the Arts. *Sylvia Lee*, coach, accompanist, Curtis Institute of Music, Philadelphia, Pennsylvania.

Information was retrieved from the Bentley Historical Library, University of Michigan (2012).

The special winter issue of *The Black Perspective in Music* (1985) contained the major speeches given at the symposium.

1) The keynote address by William C. Warfield: concert singer, professor. Mr. Warfield obtained his college education at the Eastman School of Music in Rochester, New York (bachelor of music). He also did graduate work at Eastman. He began his very important professional singing career in 1939, doing recitals and appearing in musicals such as *Call Me Mister* and the Broadway productions of Heywood's *Set My People Free* and Blitzstein's *Regina*. A highly successful town hall recital was made in 1950, and thereafter he toured in the United States and throughout the world under the sponsorship of the State Department. His appearances on stage and film in *Porgy and Bess* and *Showboat* are still highly regarded throughout the world. He has been accorded numerous honors and citations. He now serves as chairman of the Voice Department at the University of Illinois and president of the National Association of Negro Musicians.

2) "Music in the Churches of Black American: A Critical Statement" by Wendell Whalum. Dr. Wendell Phillip Whalum graduated from Booker T. Washington High School in Memphis and earned the bachelor of arts degree from Morehouse College. He received the master of arts degree from Columbia University and the PhD

degree from the University of Iowa. Since 1953, he has been professor of music in Morehouse. He is the director of the Morehouse College Glee Club, codirector of the Morehouse-Spelman Chorus, and director of music at Ebeneezer Baptist Church. He was the music director for the world premier of the opera *Treemonisha* in 1972. He is a folklorist who has published many spitituals, including, "Amazin Grace," "Roberta Lee," "Mary Had a Baby," "Mary was the Queen of Gahlee," "Sweet Jesus," "Gos is a God," and "Give Me Jesus," which are included in his publication of choral works entitled, *The Wendell P. Whalum Choral Series.*

3) "Jazz: America's Classical Music" by William "Billy" Taylor. Taylor obtained his musical education in the public schools of Washington, DC, at Virginia State College in Petersburg (bachelor of music) where he studied with Undine Smith Moore and at the University of Massachusetts at Amherst (doctor of education). In 1951, he organized the Billy Taylor Trio, which performed regularly on the night club circuit. He was also active as a radio disc jockey (1952-1966) and program director (1966-1969). In the 1970s, he founded his own company, Billy Taylor Productions. In 1965, he was cofounder of Jazzmobile in New York's Harlem community. He has published more than twelve jazz manuals.

4) "The Black American Composer and the Orchestra in the Twentieth Century" by Olly Wilson. Wilson attended St.

Louis public schools. Higher education includes a music degree from Washington University, St. Louis, Missouri; master of music degree, University of Illinois; and PhD degree, University of Iowa. He studies electronic music at the Studio for Experimental Music, University of Illinois. He has held faculty positions at Florida A & M University and Oberlin Conservatory of Music. Wilson is presently professor of music, University of California, Berkeley. His awards include Dartmouth Arts Council Prize (the first international competition for electronic compositions) for his composition "Cetus," commissioned by Boston Symphony Orchestra and Fromm Foundation for orchestral work at Tanglewood Summer 1970 entitled "Voices," and Guggenheim Fellowship for composition in 1972. He received the award for outstanding achievement in music composition from the American Academy of Arts and Letters and the National Institute of Arts and Letters in 1971. He was a visiting artist at American Academy in Rome in 1978 (volume 14, number 1, special issue).

Sidebar: 10/25/2012. I went to the historic Blue Note in New York to celebrate the eighty-sixth birthday of Jimmy Heath. His big band performed. I send Jimmy a birthday card every year. He is one of my Philadelphia legends and was part of my dissertation.

On February 26, 2006, I was honored by the Pro Arts Society along with Dr. Anna Bethal Young, William F. Douglas, and Joyce Gambrell Drayton. The affair was the 2006 Scholarship Awards Dinner Concert. It took place at Pine Memorial Baptist Church in the Frank Bernard Mitchell Hall. His son Frank Mitchell was a music magnet student at Overbrook. He is one of the leading bass baritone soloists in the area. I heard him perform the bass arias from the "Messiah" this Christmas, and I thought I was at the Met. Lynn Johnson, African American female conductor, conducted the "Black Pearl Orchestra" in this performance at Salem Baptist Church.

Pro Arts Society of Philadelphia was the brainchild of the late Julia Gilbert. She and the late Elisabeth Wilder and several musicians met and decided to organize. The name *Pro Arts Society* was suggested by Dorothy Candee, and the society was launched in 1971. The objectives of the society is to give service to the community, promote the broad spectrum of the arts, honor persons who have made outstanding contributions to the arts, and award scholarships to talented students. Past honorees are Marion Anderson, Leon Bates, Joan Myers Brown, Dr. Vivian Ford, Charles Fuller, Kenneth Goodman, Dr. Ruth Wright-Hayre, Natalie Hinderas, Sylvia Olden Lee, Charles McCabe, Trudy Pitts, Clayton White, and Camille Williams.

CHAPTER SEVENTEEN

In the summer of 2008, I received a call from Hank Hamilton, chair of the Fine Arts Department at Cheyney University of Pennsylvania. He asked if I would sub for Shirley Scott, the great musician and educator, for the fall semester. She was on medical leave. I said yes, and the fall semester lasted for eleven years. Shirley passed on March 10, 2002. I retired from the university in May 2009 as associate professor of music.

I taught the following subjects: piano class, survey of music, history of African American music, woodwind class, and music methods for elementary teachers. I also helped with the band program, which had not functioned for a number of years. Allen Gardner is the new director of bands. He began in 2007. He is doing a fine job developing the program with the help of his young family.

Sidebar: 11/3/2012. Clef Club of Jazz and Performing Arts presented the 2012 Clef Club jazz awards. Awardees were Aaron Graves, piano; Julian Pressley, alto saxophone; Robert "Bootie" Barnes, tenor saxophone; Richard Adderley, vibraphone; Leon Jordan Jr., trumpet; Brent White, trombone; Monnette Sudler, guitar; Craig McIver, percussion; Lee Smith, upright bass;

Deniece King, female vocalist; and William "TC III" Carney, male vocalist. Bootie received the Living Legend Award. Dr. Constance Clayton and Dr. Bernard Watson presented the awards. I taught or worked with many of the awardees.

I served the university in many capacities: I was member of the education committee, Virtual University Blue Ribbon Committee for the Pennsylvania State system of higher education, Academic Department Chair Workshop at Millersville State University, Faculty Academy at Penn State University; submitted and completed a strategic plan for a music curriculum; developed a web page for music methods K-6 class, NACATE Certification Committee, PECO Jazz Festival; and was director of the Honor's Arts Camp.

I performed in the following recitals on campus. On Sunday, November 20, 2005, I performed the music of Max Bruch, John Lewis of the Modern Jazz Quartet, and Duke Ellington. My son's trombone quartet, the Heritage Quartet, was the guest artist. Professor Dr. Clarence Harris played the vibraphone for the MJQ selections. Professor Allen Gardner performed with the trombone quartet. I performed Eight Pieces for Clarinet, Viola, and Piano, Op. 83, no. 1, by Max Bruch with Nina Wilkerson, a former Overbrook music magnet student, on viola and Dr. Jia An, professor of piano at Cheyney, on piano. Re-creating the MJQ with Dr. Harris on vibraphone, Tod Erkon on upright bass, Vincent Rutland on set, and me on piano, we performed "Django," "Bags Groove," "Funny Valentine," and "Blue Bossa."

The Heritage Trombone Quartet members were George E. Allen Jr., Hampton Haywood, Lionel Harwell, and Allen Gardner.

Professor of piano Toni Hall and I presented a piano duet recital on October 27, 2009, in Dudley Center for Performing Arts. The program included the following:

Concerto for Two Pianos	J. S. Bach
Third Movement from Sym. no. 1	G. Mahler
Arr.	Dr. George E. Allen
John Saw That Number—Spiritual	
Arr. A.	Westney Jr.
Improvisations—October 27, 2009	G. E. Allen
Sonata in D Major K. 448	W. A. Mozart
Movement One	
Tea for Two	V. Youmans
Arr.	M. Cornick
Stella by Starlight	Young/Washington
Arr.	G. E. Allen

Sidebar: 2/22/2012. Attended "A Tribute to Black Composers." The Cheyney University Concert Choir performed. Their conductor is Professor Marques L. A. Garrett, and they are accompanied by Professor Toni Caldwell-Hall. Concert was part of a week celebration of the founding of the university. Two of the compositions were composed by Professor Garrett, "Compensation" and the world premiere of his arrangement "My Soul's Been Anchored in the Lord."

Around 2005, to increase class participation, I started to have students do PowerPoint presentations. I divided my classes into four groups: A, B, C, and D. Each group had to have a name and a theme song that was performed before each PowerPoint presentation. Most groups chose the hip-hop genre. Some groups who had choir members composed songs. Each group picked a leader and recorder. The recorder's function was to take roll during group-working sessions in and out of class. This worked out well even when some students had to work. Groups met mainly in the library, which was a good thing, during class time. Each group had four class periods to prepare. Because we were rotating groups, this worked well. It was required that each member participate during the presentation. The other purpose for doing the project was that I noticed very little group participation in class and university activities. I asked my classes what job is there that does not involve group participation.

The project started adagio, but after students found it was fun working together, the project moved to allegro. They enjoyed working on their musical part of the presentation. I rotated groups so that group A would not always be first.

I made up the following rubric covering these areas.

Project focus
English grammar
On-time completion
Paraphrasing
Group participation

Leadership

Presentation

Originality

Excellent was 31-40 points. Good was 21-30 points. Fair was 11-20 points. Poor was 1-10 points. Most groups earned good to excellent. All presentations had to be PowerPoint. Students knew more about PowerPoint than me, but I learned quickly. *I learned from the students.*

Students had to keep a portfolio that contained all the group projects. Portfolios were handed in and graded at midterm and at the end of the semester. I would take projects to the copy center so students would have projects to put in portfolios. Projects were kept in a three-ring binder. I did not accept junk.

The other part of the grade was attendance. Attendance was important for me. I would tell my classes, "If you have a piece of paper, there is a good chance you will be hired and put on a probationary period. You must be there every day on time to become full-time." I set the example. When students come to my class, the door is open and they hear music. I always play a CD or play live on the piano. Sometimes a student would ask a question about the music. The lesson would start. The other thing I did was take attendance by number. Each student had a number. I would start by saying, "One." Class would call their numbers in order. I did this to save time because I had something to teach. I had a professor in graduate school state, "Most teachers have very little to teach." The music part of teaching was easy. The teaching for me was showing students about life through music. I could tell a lot by the music the students were making. At Cheyney University, my students made music, and these were not music majors. They sang because I *sang,* and I do not have a voice like Johnny Mathis.

When groups chose their topics, topics had to be focused. For example, a group could not do research on the life of anybody, but they could research John Coltrane's "Love Supreme" or instrumental music during the Middle Ages.

Here are sample research topics.

Famous African American Sopranos from 1970 to 1990

Jon Watson

Peter Ilyich Tchaikavsky's Musical Benefactress: Nadazhda von Meck   Aisha Willis

Ahamad Jamal's Formative Years   Shakira Currie

Childhood of Wolfgang Amadeus Mozart   Aklilu Sharp

Classical Music in Sub-Saharan Africa   Emory Peters III

The reason I had the students to have focused topics is because I was preparing them for graduate school. I told the students that if they planned to stop their education after Cheyney, they would be basically wasting their time. It is very difficult to advance in any profession with a bachelor's degree. I told students to stop using pronouns and to use *the* very little and to use *the* only if one was describing one thing, like "The one blue pencil." They might need to write Beethoven many times. For students at Cheyney, this worked. For many students, this was all they remember about the course and their group song.

When I went to Cheyney, my first class started at 9:30 a.m. I asked the chair if I could have an eight thirty class. He was reluctant at first because he said the students would not attend, but he put it on my schedule. It was my best attended class. I would arrive at seven forty-five to prepare for class and drink my decaf coffee. I would go to class at eight fifteen to open the door and put on a CD or play the piano. I would improvise in the musical style the class was learning that day.

"It is better to know than to think you know." This statement was at the beginning of all my syllabi. Ellis Marsalis, the father of Wynton, said this to me one day over the phone. I asked him if I could use the statement in my syllabi. He said yes. I would not allow my students to say "I think" or "I can't." *Can't* was not an option for my students. I got this from Dr. Madeline Cartwright, a retired teacher and administrator from Philadelphia. I invited Dr. Cartwright to come and speak to my music methods class. She is now a motivational speaker. One of the students seemed not interested in what Dr. Cartwright was saying. She stopped the presentation and said to the student, "Do you know how much money I make an hour?" She got her attention and wanted to know how much she made. Being who she was, she gave the student some ideas about making that kind of money.

I started each new class with the following statement: "Welcome to my house. We are behind. Let's get busy." I didn't wait until everybody showed up for class because at Cheyney, everybody does not make the first class. Some do not appear for two weeks, with many stories. Students have more stories than the library. I do have one story. One of my students came for two weeks, and I did not see him until a week before the finals. He stated that the reason he hadn't been to class was because his mother was pregnant and he was working a rap group. He also had a few more stories. After he finished his stories, I said to him, "If you would have attended my class, you would have noticed that the things I teach are facts. I would lay a few facts on you. One, your mother had you, and that is called experience. And two, you did not make a dime with the rap group." Conversation was over. A week later, he had put together a wonderful portfolio. He reminded me of Jonnette Newton, a student I had at Gratz, who translated the Spanish I textbook over the weekend. I did pass him. I think he learned something about rap music and the music business.

At the first class, I pass out a survey. One of the questions is "What do you plan to be doing five years from now?" Some leave the question blank. They don't know why they are at Cheyney. I tell these students, "Tell everybody you know you go to Cheyney, and the reason you are at Cheyney is to get a piece of paper." For the athletes who plan to be in the NFL and NBA, I ask them, "Why are you at Cheyney?" Many do not know the responsibilities of their positions. I would ask a football player, "What does the right guard do?" Most respond, "They block." Basketball guards respond, "They shoot?" I would give athletes extra if they came on time every day. I would do this for all students who do more than coming to class. There is one story. I had a female basketball player in my class, and she was a point guard. When I attended the games, I noticed that she would foul out of the game. So I made a deal with her. If she did not foul out in the game, I would give her $20.00. She did not foul out any more games and was not absent from class. She was a psychology major. After observing many sporting events at Cheyney, I felt that Cheyney athletes play the game but not the sport. In my eleven years at Cheyney, the football team only won maybe five games. I would tell the students, "If the coach asks you to do one hundred push-ups, you do two hundred because one hundred is only average." In America, African Americans cannot be average and have success. Academically speaking, if the math professor gives you five questions, do ten.

I had a great time at Cheyney. I only left because I needed to get a kidney transplant in 2007. I had been on dialysis for about a year and teaching. As the semester moved on, I noticed I was doing what I was telling the students not to do—be on time every day. So at the end of the semester, I told my students I was leaving to get a transplant. I received a kidney from my daughter, Robinell. It was a perfect match. My daughter told me that if I don't take care of the kidney, she is going to take it back. There is a message there. After five years with a new kidney, things are going fine. Everything works better. I celebrated my seventy-fifth birthday in December. Robinell gave me a great party.

CITATIONS/AWARDS

Director of Music at Overbrook High School in Appreciation of
Outstanding Music Instruction Given to Inner City Youth
St. Johns Settlement House April, 1980

Temple University Ester Boyer College of Music and Dance
Recognizes Participation in the Music Learning Theory Summer
Seminar July 11, 1986

For Excellent in Education Agape & B.H.B.C.
Donald Dumpson May 8, 1987

Certificate of Award
Humanitarian and Musician is a Contribution to Preservation of
African-American Classical Music
TraneStop Resource Institute, Inc. April 24, 1989

Outstanding Devotion and Limitless Creativity
Saudau-Al-Albar, Maxan Lundy,
Derrick Banks and Joan Peyton 1990

National Black Music Caucus
Outstanding Leadership and Distinguished Service to Music and
Music Education
N.B.M.C. Conference April 7, 1995

Certificate of Appreciation
Contribution to the students of all nations
Cheyney University 2002

Philadelphia Chapter Heroes Award
Recording Academy April 22, 2002

Certificate of Achievement
In Recognition for Being an Outstanding Jazz Educator
"Musicians in the Community Plus One" "Blue Monday Series"
"Artists for Education Plus One" May 26, 2003

Settlement Music School Thirteenth Annual Jeanette Selic Frank
and Blanche Wolf Ruhn Foundation Award in Recognition of
Outstanding Volunteer Service May 6, 2003

Certificate of Appreciation
In recognition of Five Years of Service
Cheyney University April 21, 2004

Founder's Club Award, Cheyney University
For Generous Support in the $1000 - $2,499 Donor Category
During the 2004 - 2005 Fiscal Year
November 11, 2005

The Pro Arts Society of Philadelphia
Distinguished Music Educator Award
Professor, Band Conductor and Instrumentalist
February 26, 2006

Overbrook High School "Hall of Fame" May 16, 2008

Settlement Music School 100
Celebrate 100 years of Excellence May 3, 2008

Alpha Phi Alpha Fraternity, Inc "Mighty" Rho Chapter in
Celebration of the 95th Anniversary
Recognition for 52 years of Service November 3, 2009

Commonwealth of Pennsylvania House of Representatives Citation
Honored upon Thirty Years of Dedication and Distinguished
Service to the Philadelphia School System
September, 10, 2009

Dr. Martin Luther King "Drum Major for Justice" Award for
Dedication and Outstanding Service
Presented by
The Fredrick Douglas Society of West
Chester University January 15, 2009

CPSIA information can be obtained at www.ICGtesting.com
Printed in the USA
BVOW08s1539070913

330584BV00004BA/299/P

9 781466 983533